Scottish Home Rule

The Answer to Scotland's Constitutional Question

Ben Thomson

BIRLINN

First published in 2020 by
Birlinn Limited
West Newington House
10 Newington Road
Edinburgh
EH9 1QS

ISBN 978 1 78027 694 6

British Library Cataloguing in Publication Data
A catalogue record for this book is available
from the British Library.

Designed and typeset by
Mark Blackadder, Edinburgh

Printed and bound by Clays Ltd, Elcograf S.p.A.

Contents

Foreword   9

Preface   11

Introduction   17

PART 1. THE HISTORY OF SCOTTISH HOME RULE

  1. Introduction   25

  2. Pre-First World War   27
     Daniel O'Connell and Catholic Emancipation   27
     Charles Stewart Parnell and Irish Home Rule   29
     Gladstone's Irish Home Rule Bills   31
     The Scottish Home Rule Association and Home Rule All Round   32
     The Liberal Party and the Government of Scotland Bill   35

  3. Post-First World War to the Establishment   37
     of the Scottish Parliament
     John MacCormick and the Birth of the Scottish National Party   37
     The Rise of the SNP and the First Devolution Referendum   40
     The Second Devolution Referendum   45
     The New Scottish Parliament and Further Constitutional Reform   52

  4. The Independence Referendum and Its Aftermath   59
     Alex Salmond and the Referendum on Independence   59
     The Smith Commission   66
     The Campaign for Scottish Home Rule   69
     Scotland Act 2016   70
     Brexit and Calls for a Second Independence Referendum   71

PART 2. THE STRUCTURE OF SCOTTISH HOME RULE

5. What Is Home Rule?   77

6. Home Rule in the Modern World   80

7. The Division of Powers   82
General Reservations   82
Specific Reservations   86

8. Financing Home Rule   102

9. Fiscal Power   106

10. The Pros and Cons of Devolving Fiscal Powers   111

11. A Fiscal Settlement for Home Rule   118

12. Social Cohesion Fund   120

13. Funding the Deficit   125

14. A Scottish Treasury   128

15. A Constitution for Home Rule   130

16. Why Home Rule Now?   134

PART 3. THE POTENTIAL OF SCOTTISH HOME RULE

17. Introduction   139

18. Reform of the Tax System   140
Making Tax Simpler   141
Three Principal Taxes   142

19. Ideas for Welfare Reform   146
Citizen's Basic Income   147
Negative Income Tax   148

20. A New Pensions System   150

21. Enhanced Local Democracy   152
    Local Financial Responsibility   153
    Reviving Local Democracy   154

22. Towards a Federal UK   156
    Federal Constitution   157
    Governance of England   157
    UK Federal Parliament   158
    Constitutional Court   160
    Constitutional Convention   160

Conclusion   162

Bibliography   164

Appendices   167

    Appendix I   167
    Summary of UK Parliament Powers Under a
    Home Rule Settlement

    Appendix II   168
    Summary of Current Scottish Parliament Powers

    Appendix III   168
    Summary of New Scottish Parliament Powers Under
    a Home Rule Settlement

Index   170

Foreword

The Rt Hon. Lord Campbell of Pittenweem CH, CBE, PC, QC, FRSE

I think I was about twelve years old and tall for my age when, in the early 1950s, I was encouraged sign the Scottish Covenant, the brain child of Dr John MacCormick, calling for Home Rule for Scotland.

In 1978 I was a small player in the Scottish Liberal team led by Russell Johnston, the long-time MP for Inverness and passionate supporter of Home Rule, which negotiated with the Labour Government represented by John Smith MP, then a Minister of State, some small changes in the Bill for a Scottish Assembly which failed to achieve the 40 per cent of the electorate hurdle in 1979.

And I stood with Charles Kennedy MP, later Leader of the Liberal Democrats, as we both signed at the same time the Claim of Right, the outcome of the constitutional convention of the late 1980s in which neither the Scottish Conservatives nor the SNP participated. Influenced by the legacy of John Smith, the Claim of Right ultimately led to the United Kingdom Parliament passing the Scotland Act of 1998 and the Scottish Parliament.

But following the Gladstone and Asquith tradition, I never lost my belief that Home Rule was and remains to this day the best and most effective and stabilising devolving of power from Westminster to Edinburgh. It's hardly surprising, therefore, that I should need no second bidding to endorse Ben Thomson's lucid, well argued and impeccably researched case for Home Rule.

At the time of writing, the political, economic and social consequences of Covid-19 are so uncertain that even the most noisy advocates of Scottish independence have felt it necessary to turn down the volume. But Thomson's assumption that at some time in the future the constitutional issue will once more be presented to the people of Scotland is hardly unreasonable.

In the negotiations led by Michael Moore MP, the then Secretary of State for Scotland, and Nicola Sturgeon, then Deputy First Minister, between Edinburgh and London, David Cameron set himself against any other choice in the 2014 referendum than a binary one.

There are those who believe that if Home Rule had been on the ballot paper it would have prevailed. Ben Thomson argues persuasively that Home Rule should be included in any future test of Scottish opinion. He does so by way of an informed account of the Home Rule movement's origins and the efforts of its supporters to promote it.

But this book is not a list of wishes. It contains detailed analysis of the fundamental issues of taxation and the division of powers between Edinburgh and London. This being Scotland, he can hardly expect unity of response. But those who accept the need for lasting and stable constitutional reform to meet the aspirations of the Scottish people and to secure Scotland's place in the United Kingdom will find much to encourage them that Home Rule is both desirable and practicable.

Menzies Campbell is the former Leader of the Liberal Democrats and Member of Parliament for North-east Fife. Since 2015 he has been a member of the House of Lords.

Preface

In my 35 years of business I have seen many management styles. Generally, however, managers and their organisations fall into two camps: the first favours heavy centralisation and getting things done through a chain of command, while the second favours delegated management, with responsibility devolved to those in charge of the relevant part of the business. I have always and unashamedly been in the second of these camps. Fundamentally, I believe that people will rise to the job if they are given responsibility within an organisation and allowed to stand on their own two feet. As this book will demonstrate, it is this principle that has guided my support for Scottish Home Rule.

Of course, sometimes it is risky to delegate, and sometimes people may let you down, making good guidance and support all the more important. And, yes, often the person with greater experience could have done a task faster, but doing so would have meant denying others the experience they needed to improve. Overall, though, my own management career has been amply rewarded by seeing so many people rise to the responsibilities they have been given.

I have long been interested in politics, and between school and university I worked as a researcher in the House of Commons. Government at any level involves a wonderful (and sometimes not-so-wonderful!) mix of people, ideas and beliefs. Everyone can and should contribute. Over the years, I have been fortunate enough to meet and debate with politicians from all major parties, and through advising government have been able to gain insight into how it operates. It has always struck me how similar the structure and management of business organisations and government is. In my assessment, government errs towards centralisation and so struggles to delegate – this applies across the board, from the civil service executive who carries out public sector work to the various local and community levels of government. Arguments regarding organisation often heard in large centralised businesses are echoed in Westminster: the quality of local politicians not good enough and blame comes back to the top, so the top must manage things.

In 2007, I stepped down after ten years as CEO of the Scottish Investment Bank Noble Group and became its part-time chairman. This gave me time to do other things, including becoming Chairman of the National Galleries of Scotland, a job I enjoyed for eight years and showed me at close quarters how public sector organisations can inspire people and change lives. I also became involved in advising Scottish government in a number of ways. I had been a director of Scottish Financial Enterprise and, together with its chair, John Campbell, persuaded the then First Minister, Lord McConnell, to set up the Financial Services Advisory Board (FiSAB) to liaise between Scottish government and the financial sector. I served on its board for the first five years. Separately, I advised Scottish government on the situation facing Scottish banks during the 2008 banking crisis, particularly HBOS. In 2010, I produced the Thomson Review on reforms to representation in the Scottish Courts, and also went on to chair the board of Creative Scotland, Scotland's arts and film funding body. These roles provided me with insight into the interface between the commercial sectors and government, setting me along the path to setting up and subsequently chairing Reform Scotland, a non-party-aligned think tank tasked with helping research and promoting public policy. I was encouraged in this by senior politicians of all parties, who saw the value of such an organisation in the relatively new Scottish Parliament.

I set up Reform Scotland in 2008 together with Geoff Mawdsley, who was its director for the first ten years. Its stated aim was to set out a better way of delivering increased economic prosperity and more effective public services, based on the traditional Scottish principles of limited government, diversity and personal responsibility. Fundamental to this was a belief that government is best served by devolving responsibility to whichever level of government is best able to deliver a particular public service. It gained support from individuals within all the political parties in Scotland. As Alex Salmond, the First Minister at the time, said at our first annual dinner: 'I agree strongly with about a third of what Reform Scotland says, I am okay with about a third and I disagree with about a third, which is probably about right for an independent think tank.'

Although Reform Scotland initially focused mainly on public sector areas, such as education, health, policing and transport, it soon became impossible to ignore the constitutional debate in Scotland. Given Reform Scotland's focus on limited government, diversity and personal responsibility, it seemed natural that it should promote a Home Rule-type option, with Scotland having more domestic matters passed to its control while remaining part of the UK. Therefore, in 2010, based on a report we had written as evidence to the Calman Commission and the Scottish government's National Conversation campaign, we set up the Campaign for Fiscal Responsibility. The group, which I chaired, aimed to build a broad coalition in support of the Scottish Parliament gaining greater financial responsibility.

With the 2011 election of the majority Scottish National Party (SNP) government, the political debate in Scotland underwent a sea-change. No longer was it a debate over more powers, it was a debate about independence. As a result, the Campaign for Fiscal Responsibility ended and the debate moved on. In 2011, Reform Scotland published 'Devolution Plus', setting out our evidence to the Scotland Bill Committee and outlining a new tax and spending framework. This included the devolution not only of sufficient taxes to ensure the Scottish government would be responsible for raising what it spent, but also of benefits linked to such policy areas as housing and social inclusion. In February 2012, I set up and chaired the Devo Plus Group, which was initially led by former Lib Dem MSP Jeremy Purvis. The group consisted of high-profile politicians from each of the unionist parties (Liberal Democrats, Conservatives and Labour), who all believed that more powers should be devolved to Holyrood while at the same time Scotland should remain within the UK. The purpose of the group was to promote the idea of greater devolution within the parties, in the hope that the public would have a clearer idea of exactly what would happen after the referendum in the event of a 'No' vote.

A year before the referendum, the Devo Plus Group called on all the unionist parties to sign a 'Glasgow Agreement' setting out the foundation for how further powers would be devolved in the event of a 'No' vote. We also published polling, carried out by YouGov, indicating that 16 per cent of voters who did not currently plan on voting 'No' were more likely to do so if this led to substantially more powers being devolved to Holyrood.

Alongside this, I was persuading the First Minister, Alex Salmond, to push for a second question in the referendum, offering a choice between the status quo and devolving the majority of fiscal powers under a Devo Plus or Devo Max scheme. While the Scottish government backed this proposal, it proved a red line for British Prime Minister David Cameron in the 2012 Edinburgh Agreement negotiations, which set out the terms of the referendum. This was both a huge shame and a missed opportunity.

At the time, the Prime Minister, believing he had a comfortable majority to win the referendum, did not want to confuse a straight fight between the status quo and independence. In the final couple of weeks leading up to the referendum, however, the result looked less certain and he was forced to concede the middle ground through the 'vow'. This vow, formulated by Gordon Brown and agreed by all the unionist party leaders, laid out a set of ideas for a federal-like arrangement after the referendum. While it is hard to know how much this influenced voters, many think this offer of an alternative federalist option was a key factor in Scotland remaining within the union.

Following the referendum, I wanted to ensure the vow was honoured in a way that was fully reflective of the promises made by the unionist party leaders. I therefore helped set up and chaired the Campaign for Scottish Home Rule (CSHR). This involved people associated with the five main political parties in Scotland, as well as others from outside traditional party politics. Its aim was to submit a report to the Smith Commission, which had been set up to implement the vow, and ensure it stayed true to the promises made.

CSHR believed the Home Rule settlement had to be based on clear principles. As such, it set out the following three guiding principles:

- **Devolve responsibilities:** A presumption in favour of devolving responsibilities to Holyrood, with a review of Schedule 5 of the Scotland Act 1998 and the burden of proof resting with Westminster should it wish to retain a responsibility.
- **Raise what you spend:** Ensure both Holyrood and Westminster have the appropriate tax and borrowing powers to make them responsible for raising the money they spend.
- **Mutual respect:** Improve the relationship between parliaments and secure the permanence of the Scottish Parliament, which would almost certainly require a written constitution (or something similar) for the UK.

The CSHR's view of the eventual Smith Commission recommendations was that not only did they fail to meet these principles, they were essentially based on no underlying principle or principles. Instead, they were the outcome of political horse-trading arising from the different party proposals. Ultimately, this meant the solution was unlikely to be either sustainable or stable, as it was not built on a consensus about the type of Home Rule settlement the people of Scotland wanted or needed. This was deeply disappointing, given the strength of the promises made by the unionist parties.

It is not always easy to occupy the middle ground. The independence referendum polarised political opinion into two camps: all or nothing. It cost me friends on both sides, who believed in the old adage that if you are not with us you are against us. The day before the referendum, when the stakes were at their highest, senior politicians on both sides tried to twist my arm into declaring that Reform Scotland would support their camp. We did not, as Reform Scotland's alternative proposition of a Home Rule-type settlement was not merely a compromise, but a path that I believed offered a better way for Scotland and the UK to work in collaboration. It is also a path that I continue to believe many voters would support, and should be on any ballot in the event of another referendum. Before this can happen, though, its principles and practicalities need to be clearly laid out, and the ultimate aim of federalism robustly defended. This, then, is why I have written the book you now hold in your hands: Home Rule is a way forward I passionately and wholeheartedly believe in. Hopefully, the following pages will demonstrate why this is the case.

Introduction

The concept of Home Rule is not always clearly understood, and has often been misrepresented – sometimes inadvertently, sometimes deliberately. What it does demonstrate, however, is the potency of the idea as a label under which groups and individuals have attempted to package their preferred set of constitutional proposals. Above all, it is important to understand that Home Rule is distinct from both independence and current devolved government. Only if this distinction is more widely understood will we be able to enable in a fully informed debate on the constitutional options available to Scotland and the UK as a whole.

The specifics of Home Rule can be defined in many ways, but for the purposes of this book two characteristics are key. Firstly, Scotland and UK must be a constitutionally mandated partnership of equals; and, secondly, Scotland must have responsibility for all areas of policy unless the burden of proof suggests otherwise. While devolution can in theory deliver on the second point, it can never do so for the first. Also, though Home Rule has potential implications for a federal UK, it is not itself federalism, as this book will explain.

It should be acknowledged that Home Rule has its opponents on both sides of the fence. Those who support unionism often see Home Rule as a slippery slope to independence, while those who support independence see it as a unionist proposal to retain sovereignty over Scotland. Donald Dewar is often given credit for the famous phrase 'devolution is a process not an event' (in actual fact, it was first coined by former Welsh Secretary Ron Davies). Yet this statement is not entirely helpful, as it suggests that passing powers to Scotland inevitably leads to independence, with Home Rule merely a step along the way. It need not be. Home Rule is a destination in its own right, or if it is a stepping stone then it is just as likely to lead to federalism. The history of Home Rule is also different from independence, with roots that go all the way back to the second half of the 19th century and the formation of the Scottish Home Rule Association.

Understanding the concept of Home Rule is more important than ever, as it is clear that the question of Scotland's constitutional future is far from settled. This is despite the fact that in the Edinburgh Agreement – which determined how the 2014 independence referendum should be conducted – both sides portrayed the referendum as a 'once in a generation' decision. Yet, by March 2017, the Scottish government had submitted a Section 30 request to its UK counterpart, which would give the Scottish Parliament the legal power to hold an independence referendum. Several factors led to this, the most significant being Brexit. In the Brexit referendum of June 2016, 52 per cent of people in the UK as a whole voted to leave the European Union (EU), while in Scotland only 38 per cent did so. This difference in attitude towards the EU was the main justification for the Scottish government pursuing another referendum, supported by the Scottish Parliament, which – through the combination of SNP and Green MSPs – has a majority in favour of independence. The protracted difficulties with the Brexit negotiations, the existence of a significant number of SNP MPs at Westminster, Boris Johnson succeeding Theresa May as Prime Minister, the strong performance of the SNP in the December 2019 election, and the subsequent departure of the UK from the EU at the end of January 2020, have all served to intensify these calls for another Scottish referendum.

If another referendum is to happen, it is important that people in Scotland are not restricted to the options of independence and the status quo, but are also offered Home Rule. The fact that the current devolved settlement has not created a genuine partnership of equals between Scotland and the rest of the UK has understandably fostered resentment amongst many. This has been compounded by Home Rule being largely absent from the discussion, leading to a polarised debate between the opposing status quo and independence camps. Thus, we are at a crossroads. If the path of maintaining the current devolved settlement is taken, this risks creating a still greater sense of resentment amongst half the Scottish population. Equally, if the path towards full independence is pursued, this means going against the strongly held views of the other half of the population. There is, though, another way forward, one that attempts to achieve a broader consensus. It requires a two-question referendum, which would allow voters to decide not only whether sovereignty should reside at either Holyrood or Westminster, but whether or not they would prefer Home Rule – with sovereignty split between the two levels of government – to either of these options.

At its heart, the disagreement between unionism and independence is a battle over sovereignty. In other words, should the ultimate power to make political decisions lie with Westminster or Holyrood? However, despite sovereignty being much loved by politicians and political analysts, it is a somewhat vague and indistinct concept for most of the public. We increasingly live in a world where decisions are taken at many different levels and – particularly for younger people – allegiance to a single ultimate affinity group is something of an antiquated concept. Many of us feel perfectly comfortable supporting UK athletics, Scottish rugby and even Barcelona at football, without feeling the need to prioritise one over the other. Even so, as we have seen in recent years, such concepts as sovereignty and national identity can be unsettling for older generations and their sense of identity in an increasingly globalised world.

Home Rule has always been about decentralising control of local matters (or what used to be called domestic matters) while remaining part of a wider entity. It is a form of government in which the responsibilities of national government and those of sub-national government are clearly separated. Crucially, a genuine Home Rule settlement requires constitutional checks and balances ensuring that the relationship between the national and sub-national level is mutually respected, and that any changes to the relationship are mutually agreed.

Home Rule is a bilateral arrangement between one area within a nation state and the rest of that nation state. This is distinct from federalism, which represents an equal relationship between *all* constituent parts of a country. There is no obvious reason why a Home Rule settlement cannot be sustained over the long term, although it is true that campaigns for Home Rule can lead to independence, as happened in Ireland. In Ireland's case, however, this was – at least partly – due to a failure to deliver meaningful Home Rule. If Home Rule proves successful it could provide a template for the entire UK moving towards full federalism, with each constituent part responsible for domestic matters. In this regard, it is worth noting that some of the most economically successful countries in the world are run as federal nations, including the USA, Switzerland, Germany and Australia.

For much of the 130 or so years since the Scottish Home Rule Association was formed, Home Rule was a movement in its own right, largely separate in its aims and objectives from movements centred around independence. In 1914, a bill brought by a Liberal MP to establish Home Rule in Scotland passed its second reading in the House of Commons. Sadly, it was never enacted due to the outbreak of the First World War, after which the Liberals lost and then never regained power.

Given this, it seems somewhat strange that in the run-up to the 2014 independence referendum, Home Rule was largely ignored, or, at best, discussed as a compromise position. In negotiations between David Cameron and Alex Salmond for the Edinburgh Agreement, the Scottish government's negotiating team did in fact put a two-question referendum on the table. The first question asked whether Scotland should have independence, while the second asked, should independence be rejected, whether Scotland should have Devo Max (the SNP's version of Home Rule, even if it differs in some important respects to Home Rule as it is proposed in this book). It proved to be David Cameron's only real red line in the negotiations. He accepted lowering the voting age to 16, which was thought to benefit the independence cause, and allowed the independence question to be framed as a 'Yes' for independence and 'No' for the status quo – again, an important concession to the SNP. However, despite polls at the time indicating it would have been the most popular choice, he would not move on including Devo Max as a third option.

The first part of this book sets out the background and history of the Scottish Home Rule movement and its relationship with Irish Home Rule. It is a history that is separate from the independence movement, although at times the two are interconnected. The book will also show how the precise meaning of the term Home Rule – while always lying somewhere between the complete sovereignty of Westminster and the complete transfer of sovereignty to a Scottish Parliament – has shifted throughout its history.

Part two looks at the current constitutional relationship between Scotland and the UK, before setting out what a defined structure of Home Rule could look like and why this would lead to a new and better relationship. It also examines how responsibilities should be split between Scotland and the rest of the UK; how a Home Rule settlement should be financed and what fiscal powers would be required; and how current constitutional arrangements would need to be changed in order to deliver a genuine partnership of equals.

Finally, part three examines the potential of Home Rule, including how such a settlement between Scotland and the rest of the UK might develop into a fully federal system. Further, it explores what might be done with the new powers devolved under Home Rule, and how they could be used to strengthen Scotland both economically and socially, including improving public sector services.

Despite devolution, the UK is still in many ways a centralised country due to the high level of fiscal control exerted by Westminster. It is not only Scotland, or even Wales and Northern Ireland, that would like to see more powers devolved in order to bring decision-making closer to those affected – many local areas, such as Manchester or London, feel this way too. While national governments are often keen to publicly espouse this principle, known as 'subsidiarity', they tend to be less enthusiastic about devolving powers in practice. This has resulted in a strong desire for greater devolution and, in Scotland, a simmering dissatisfaction with the status quo.

At the same time, full independence comes attached with real problems, with monetary policy being one of the independence campaign's most unconvincing arguments in the run-up to the 2014 referendum. If Scotland were to leave the UK, what currency should it use? To continue using sterling without any mechanisms for influencing monetary policy was seen as a weakness, yet the alternative of moving to a Scottish currency or the euro was not popular with the majority of voters, with only around 12 per cent supporting it.

The stated rationale for a second independence referendum is that people in Scotland, contrary to the rest of the UK (Northern Ireland excepted), voted to remain within the EU. This was backed up by the SNP's strong performance in the December 2019 UK general election. Thus, it is logical to assume that should there be a majority vote for independence, Scotland will immediately apply to re-join the EU, and as a new member will be part of the euro currency. While the public may change its views on the euro, this is certainly an obstacle to independence.

However, there is now a larger problem that events since the last independence referendum have created. If the UK leaves the EU there are likely to be tariffs and hard borders, which will have a major impact on trade and the movement of people. Currently, 60 per cent of Scotland's trade is with the rest of the UK, compared to 19 per cent with EU countries. As an EU member, Scotland will be bound to the same trading arrangements with the UK as the EU's other members. Any disruption of trade with the UK would have a major economic impact on Scotland, which would inevitably be more damaging than any barriers to trade with the EU that Brexit might create for Scotland as part of the UK. In addition, if there was a need for a hard border, this would have serious implications for the many families with relatives and friends on both sides of the border.

Home Rule should not be seen as a compromise between independence and the status quo – rather, it is a proposal in its own right which provides most of the benefits of both. Under Home Rule, the Scottish government would have responsibility for domestic matters, including the setting and collection of taxes, social welfare, pensions, drug enforcement, and many other issues. However, Scots under Home Rule would still be UK citizens, with monetary policy (including borrowing), international relations, defence and trade decided by the UK government, albeit with input from the Scottish government. In addition, there would be a mutually agreed constitution, changes to which would require the consent of both levels of government.

This book's primary focus is to set out how Home Rule might work for Scotland, in doing so demonstrating that it is the best way – indeed, perhaps the only way – of resolving longstanding tensions and ensuring a better relationship between Scotland and the rest of the UK. This new relationship would be a genuine partnership of equals, with the UK only responsible for those areas where a UK-wide policy was essential or beneficial, leaving maximum scope for Scottish policies to meet the needs of Scottish people. This would create a partnership founded on mutual gain, providing a solid basis for greater prosperity and social cohesion. It could also serve as a model for other parts of the UK – such as Wales, Northern Ireland or regions of England – that might wish to adopt elements of it. In time, it may even prompt a move to a fully-fledged federal structure for the UK as a whole. Ultimately, though, a federal UK is something that all UK citizens must decide on – such constitutional changes cannot, and should not, be forced on others simply because people in Scotland think they are a good idea.

Similarly, this book is not about forcing people to agree with the idea of Scottish Home Rule. Rather, its purpose is to put this option on the table, enabling readers to fully understand a path that has been conveniently ignored by those who would prefer a polarised debate between the current devolved settlement and independence. Home Rule represents a clear proposal with its own end point and, most importantly, its own underlying philosophy. It is a choice that acknowledges we live in a global world, while also recognising that local communities want greater responsibility for local matters, and to be able to stand on their own feet.

PART I
THE HISTORY OF SCOTTISH
HOME RULE

I
Introduction

In the words of Danish philosopher Søren Kierkegaard, 'Life can only be understood backwards; but it must be lived forwards.' If the history of constitutional change has taught us anything, it is that it is constantly evolving. In terms of Scotland's history, two differing philosophies have co-existed alongside each other – sometimes clearly distinct, sometimes confused. The first is the philosophy of nationalism. The independence movement is about Scotland becoming a fully independent nation with the sovereignty to make its own decisions. Although supporters of independence point to the economic and social benefits this will bring, at its core is an emotive belief that power should lie with the people of Scotland. This is the driving principle behind the Scottish National Party. On the other side of this coin, the unionist movement rest on an equally emotive belief: the Scottish people are citizens of the United Kingdom and have long benefited from being in this union. Thus, why change now? There is currently a more equal split in the Scottish population between these two beliefs than at any time in the past two centuries.

The second philosophy is one of decentralisation. This involves the principle of subsidiarity, in which decisions are taken as close as possible to where they will have their effect, with central government only performing those tasks that cannot be performed at a more local level. This principle – which drives devolution, federalism and Home Rule – has gained supporters across all the main political parties, including the SNP. At times during the last hundred years, organisations have been set up by Labour, and by the Liberals, as well as right-of-centre groups, to campaign for Home Rule or federalism.

What is clear is that Home Rule is a distinct end point in its own right rather than necessarily being a stepping stone to independence. It should therefore be evaluated on this basis when being compared with the alternative constitutional options of a devolved Scottish Parliament or independence.

This distinction between Home Rule and independence is apparent from the history of the various campaigns for greater Scottish self-government, which is why some understanding of this history is vital. Initially, it was inspired by the Irish Home Rule movement, which is why it is worth knowing what that movement demanded. However, after the First World War a divergence emerged between those who wanted greater control over Scottish affairs within the UK and those who wanted full independence. This division continues to this day, despite the two camps having worked together, albeit uneasily, at various points along the way – most notably in the two referendums on Scottish devolution.

2

Pre-First World War

Daniel O'Connell and Catholic Emancipation

The roots of Scottish Home Rule can be found in the Irish Home Rule movement. In the early part of the 19th century, the dominant figure in this movement was Daniel O'Connell. O'Connell hailed from the west of Ireland and, according to historian Brian Igoe, was born in 1775 into a native Irish family who had been rulers in County Kerry for centuries. As Catholics, they were outside the Protestant Ascendancy – made up of members of the established Church of Ireland or Church of England – which dominated Ireland at this time.

As was their tradition, O'Connell's parents arranged for him brought up as a foster child in the family of his father's head cowman. This was to ensure that he learnt how to deal with hardships, and also became familiar with local traditions, folklore practices and the Irish language. He was later adopted by his childless uncle, who was the head of their clan, and was sent along with his brother to France to study. This was because, as a Catholic, he could not attend universities in Ireland, England or Scotland. While there, the French Revolution broke out and O'Connell and his brother were forced to leave for London.

The perceived unfairness of British rule in Ireland was the major driver of both the move towards enhanced rights for Catholics and the later Home Rule movement. For O'Connell, the obstacles placed in the way of Catholics must have been a key driver of his desire to see reform and an end to such injustices. For example, prior to the Catholic Relief Act of 1791, Catholics had been prevented from practising law. The act removed some of the restrictions facing Catholics and allowed O'Connell to study at schools in Dublin and London, following which he was admitted to the Irish Bar in 1798.

That same year saw rebellions against British rule in Ireland by Wolfe Tone and the Society of United Irishmen. Historian Robert McNamara believes that O'Connell read many of the great Enlightenment writers – such as Voltaire, Rousseau and Thomas Paine – during his time in France, and that he later became friendly with the English philosopher Jeremy Bentham. On top of his lack of approval for British rule in Ireland, he was, therefore, sympathetic to radical and reforming ideas. Despite this, O'Connell was opposed to open revolt, partly due to what he had witnessed in France during the revolution, but also because he feared the consequences of such rebellion. In this he was proved right, as the rebellion was crushed in the most brutal manner.

This served to harden O'Connell's opposition to violent revolution. Thus, in the early 19th century campaign for Catholic emancipation, he used existing political structures and peaceful methods to achieve his goals. He was, by all accounts, a gifted orator and charismatic figure, using these attributes – along with his skills as a lawyer – to secure enhanced rights for the Catholic population. In the 1820s, he turned the Irish Catholic Association into a widespread political organisation seeking Catholic emancipation. In 1828, he was elected as an MP, although, as a Catholic, he was unable to take his seat in the House of Commons. However, the campaign was ultimately successful and resulted in the Roman Catholic Relief Act passing in 1829, which removed most of the major remaining restrictions placed on Roman Catholics, including being able to sit in the House of Commons.

Following the success of his campaign, O'Connell turned his attention to repealing the 1801 Act of Union, which had merged the parliaments of Great Britain and Ireland. He set up the Repeal Association, arguing for an independent kingdom of Ireland, with Queen Victoria remaining as monarch. The Repeal Association's main tactic was to hold large meetings across much of Ireland. At one of these meetings, held at Drogheda in June 1843, O'Connell set out his objective: 'I want to make all Europe and America know it – I want to make England feel her weakness if she refuses to give the justice we the Irish require – the restoration of our domestic parliament ...'

These meetings proved to be a cause of concern for the British government, with Sir Robert Peel banning a meeting at Clontarf in 1843. O'Connell, who agreed to call off the meeting, was fined and imprisoned for conspiracy, though he was released after three months when the conviction was quashed by the House of Lords. This ended the influence of the Repeal Association, confirmed by the death of Daniel O'Connell in 1847.

O'Connell was in many ways a controversial figure. Not only was he rumoured to have had many affairs and children out of wedlock, he fought a duel which ended with a man dying. He was also resented by those who wanted to see a more full-blooded and violent response to what they saw as intolerable British rule in Ireland. While this split between those favouring more violent revolution and those favouring reform would persist, O'Connell remains a key figure in Irish history, as it was his example that inspired Charles Stewart Parnell and others to seek Home Rule for Ireland rather than take the route to independence. Perhaps the greatest tribute to O'Connell was paid by William Gladstone, who called him the 'greatest popular leader the world has ever seen'.

Charles Stewart Parnell and Irish Home Rule

In the latter part of the 19th century, O'Connell's mantle as Ireland's foremost political leader passed to Charles Stewart Parnell. As Robert McNamara points out, Parnell was an unlikely nationalist leader. A Protestant landowner, he was born in 1846 to a family who were part of the Anglo-Irish gentry, and so were beneficiaries of the landlord system imposed on Ireland by British rule. However, Parnell's family had opposed the Act of Union with Britain and supported Catholic emancipation, and his American mother held staunchly anti-British views.

Parnell became a supporter of Home Rule for Ireland – a term first used in relation to Ireland in the 1860s. It referred to a body that would legislate on domestic affairs and was increasingly seen as part of a federal system for the UK, with an Imperial Parliament at Westminster and an Irish Parliament in Dublin. This contrasted with the views of groups such as the Fenians and Irish Republican Brotherhood, which wanted complete independence from Britain, by force if necessary.

In 1870, the Irish Home Government Association was formed, becoming in turn the Home Rule League in 1873. Its aim was a limited form of self-government within the United Kingdom. The Home Rule movement began running candidates for Parliament and in 1875 Parnell was elected in a by-election in County Meath. The fact that he was a Protestant was felt by some to give the Home Rule cause greater respectability. Once in Parliament, however, he enthusiastically adopted more radical tactics than many of his colleagues had anticipated. This included obstructing parliamentary legislation as a means of making the British people and government take note of Irish complaints. Such tactics were effective, though some felt they risked turning the British public against the cause of Irish Home Rule.

In 1879, Parnell became president of the National Land League, financed by Irish Americans with the aim of ending landlordism. The 1880 election saw the Home Rulers win 63 of 103 Irish seats. Charles Stewart Parnell became chairman and the grouping became an increasing force in Parliament. Gladstone responded to the activities of the National Land League by introducing the 1881 Land Act, which gave Irish tenant farmers secure tenures at fair rents. This, however, did not satisfy Parnell, who was imprisoned for encouraging agrarian disturbances. He was released under what was known as the 'Kilmainham Treaty', in which Parnell promised to renounce violence and the Liberal government promised to improve the Land Act. The latter was offered in return for the Home Rulers' support in the government's attempts to solve the Irish question.

Having flirted with a more violent, extra-parliamentary approach to addressing Ireland's problems, Parnell changed his focus to strengthening parliamentary representation in order to promote the cause of Home Rule. He turned the League into a formal party – the Irish Parliamentary Party – and used Irish American money to pay for talented and committed people to stand for Parliament. This resulted in the Irish Parliamentary Party winning 85 of 103 Irish seats at the 1885 election. He used this newfound parliamentary strength to start a bidding war between the Conservatives and Liberals for Irish Party support. Gladstone's offer of Home Rule was the clincher, leading to his failed first Home Rule Bill, described below.

In the late 1880s, Parnell was at the height of his power and influence, having united a broad spectrum of nationalist opinion in Ireland around his preferred vision of a constitutional and parliamentary route to Home Rule. Sadly, this all ended abruptly following the revelation of Parnell's affair with a married woman, Katherine O'Shea, during her husband's divorce proceedings. The contrast with the treatment of his predecessor Daniel O'Connell – whose career was largely untouched by rumours of multiple affairs – is stark. In Parnell's case, the very public scandal saw him deserted by a majority of those in his own Irish Parliamentary Party, as well as by the Liberals. He stood down as leader in 1890, trying desperately but unsuccessfully to resurrect his career in a series of by-elections. The exertion took its toll on his health and he died in 1891.

Gladstone's Irish Home Rule Bills

The conversion of Gladstone and the Liberals to the cause of Home Rule for Ireland did not take place overnight. Upon being told that he had become Prime Minister after the 1868 election, Gladstone famously broke off from chopping trees at his house to declare, 'My mission is to pacify Ireland.'

As historian Michael Morrogh has pointed out, prior to this Gladstone had shown little concern for the problems of those in Ireland, his interest only having been sparked by the Fenian rising of 1867 and subsequent terrorism on the British mainland in 1868. He had then read extensively on the subject and, initially, was unsympathetic to Irish Home Rule. Instead, he thought that the problems of Ireland could be solved by addressing the various social grievances of its people, in particular those relating to the Church, land and education.

Thus, Gladstone disestablished the Church of Ireland, which had similar rights and lands as in England, despite not representing the vast majority of Ireland's population, who were Catholic. Indeed, it did not even represent many Protestants, who were mainly Presbyterian dissenters in the north. This act united his party and was deemed a success. He then moved on to land reform with the 1870 Irish Land Act, which gave tenants greater security but did not address rent control. However, problems arose once more in relation to land, with the agricultural depression in 1879 exploited by Parnell. Despite another Land Act in 1881, Morrogh argues that Gladstone realised his aim of heading off calls for political change in Ireland by social reform was destined to fail.

Gladstone's motives for shifting his party to support Irish Home Rule have been much debated. Some see it as merely opportunism, as it enabled him to gain the support of the Irish Parliamentary Party and so oust the Conservatives from government. However, Morrogh points to fresh evidence from Gladstone's diaries and other material, which show that he had come to accept the justice of Home Rule and saw no other alternative. In essence, Gladstone felt he should support the democratic choice of people in Ireland, just as he had done in other European countries, such as Italy and Germany. All other methods had proven unsuccessful both in pacifying Ireland and ending calls for Home Rule.

Thus, despite the damage inflicted on his party and its unpopularity in Britain, Gladstone sought a long-term political settlement based on Home Rule. This led to the first Home Rule Bill for Ireland in 1886, which proposed a single chamber assembly in Dublin, with all Irish MPs excluded from Westminster. Westminster would retain control over a range of issues, including defence, treaties with foreign states, trade and coinage.

The bill itself was put together in a rush, leading to the jibe that Gladstone was 'an old man in a hurry'. Despite thinking it flawed, Parnell was prepared to vote for the bill. However, there was no attempt to persuade those in Britain of the merits of the legislation, with the predominant view being that it would lead to the break-up of the United Kingdom and the Empire. This was also the view of the majority in Parliament. As a result, the bill was defeated in the House of Commons and caused Liberal Unionists, such as Joseph Chamberlain, to leave the party and ally themselves with the Conservatives.

Having lost power, Gladstone was unable to present another Home Rule bill until 1893. As with the first bill, it was drafted in secret by Gladstone himself, without input from the Irish Parliamentary Party. By this time, the Irish Parliamentary Party had split into two factions – those who had been for its leader Charles Stewart Parnell, who had died two years earlier, and those who had been against.

The Second Home Rule Bill proposed an Irish Parliament with two separate chambers and, unlike the first bill, allowed for 80 Irish MPs to vote at Westminster. Despite passing the House of Commons, the bill was heavily defeated in the House of Lords, which was controlled by the Conservative Party. Gladstone retired soon afterwards.

The Scottish Home Rule Association and Home Rule All Round

Prior to 1707, and stretching back to the early 13th century, Scotland had had its own Parliament. The Act of Union ended this, turning the independent kingdoms of Scotland and England (along with Wales) into Great Britain, under a single legislature. This was followed in 1801 by the Union with Ireland Act, which formed the United Kingdom of Great Britain and Ireland.

In the early part of the 19th century, in contrast to Ireland, there was no great discontent in Scotland driving a demand for increased self-government. One reason for this was the generally strong performance of the economy. Another was that the Victorian state was not particularly centralised, which enabled the Scottish middle class to exercise a considerable degree of self-government. However, historians have also pointed to the dominance of something Graeme Morton calls 'unionist-nationalism', with Naomi Lloyd-Jones explaining: 'Although a seemingly oxymoronic term, "Unionist-nationalism" has helped to make sense of the landscape of 19th-century Scottish political culture. It denotes a belief that the Union with England enabled Scots to express their nation's distinctive attributes within a wider British and imperial framework.' This attitude stressed that the fact that, unlike in Wales, the Union had maintained important Scottish institutions, such as the Church, the education system and Scots law – all key elements of Scottish national identity.

Despite the dominance of this attitude, the Scottish Home Rule movement did not appear from nowhere, as dissatisfaction with the constitutional system had existed for some time. In the 1850s, the National Association for the Vindication of Scottish Rights was formed. It did not call for a Scottish Parliament, but focused instead on securing a fairer deal for Scotland from the Treasury, as well as better administration and governance. Its campaign led to the Scottish Office and the post of Secretary for Scotland being reinstated in 1885, their purpose being to promote Scotland's interests and express concerns to the UK government. The post had existed for almost 40 years following the Act of Union, but was abolished in 1746, with the Home Secretary becoming formally responsible for Scottish affairs and the Lord Advocate carrying out much of the actual work. The reinstatement was a recognition of Scottish identity's political dimension and was perhaps a response to a growing feeling within the country that it was being neglected in comparison with Ireland.

The increasing focus on Ireland and the attendant constitutional crisis continued to drive demands for Scottish Home Rule. The key organisation promoting greater self-government in Scotland was the Scottish Home Rule Association, founded in 1886, a month after Gladstone introduced the first Irish Home Rule Bill. A number of notable individuals were involved in the Association, including eventual Labour leaders Keir Hardie and Ramsay MacDonald, and Robert Cunninghame Graham, described by former SNP MP George Kerevan as 'arguably the most colourful figure to enter the Commons in the past 200 years'. Cunninghame Graham was a founder and first president of both the Labour Party and later the SNP, though this was perhaps one of the less surprising aspects of his life, as a House of Commons early day motion tabled on on 1 March 2016 reveals:

... this house remembers RB Cunninghame Graham who was first elected to Parliament in 1886 and who died on 20 March 1936; notes that he was a Scottish politician, writer, journalist and adventurer, that he entered Parliament as a radical Liberal Party member standing on a platform of the abolition of the House of Lords, Scottish Home Rule, universal suffrage and an eight-hour working day, that he was suspended from the House in December 1888 for protesting about the working conditions of chain-makers and that his response to the Speaker of the House, 'I never withdraw' was used later by George Bernard Shaw in *Arms and the Man*; and further notes that he became the first-ever socialist hon. Member of Parliament, first president of the Scottish Labour Party, a founder member of the National Party of Scotland in 1928 and first president of the Scottish National Party in 1934.

Edinburgh historian Nathan Kane sets out the four founding objectives of the Scottish Home Rule Association as: 'To maintain integrity of the empire, secure a Scottish legislature for purely Scottish matters, maintain Scotland's position within the Imperial Parliament and foster national sentiment.' In furthering these objectives, the Association used arguments similar to those made more recently for devolution or independence. Naomi Lloyd-Jones has detailed some of these, including supporting the passage of 'legislation for Scotland in Scotland', using the term Home Rule 'to express shortly the right of the Scottish people to manage their own affairs', and arguing only a reinstated legislature could 'carry out what the people of Scotland want' for 'the Scottish people know their own business best'. In keeping with its founding objectives, it is important to understand that the Association did not advocate outright independence, though it no doubt included people who sought this goal. Lloyd-Jones refers to its vice-chairman, John Romans, who is quoted as saying: 'No Scotsman, whose opinion is worth repeating, entertains for a moment, an approximation to repeal of the Union.'

Alongside these appeals was the more straightforward argument that a Scottish legislature would provide more time for the discussion of Scottish issues. These, it was felt, were often squeezed out at Westminster, particularly in light of the increasing focus on Ireland. A further argument used by the Association was that was that if Home Rule for Ireland resulted in a separate Irish legislature as well as Irish representation at Westminster, this would mean the Irish could interfere in Scottish affairs while Scottish MPs would have no role in Irish affairs. The Association thought the best and fairest way to address this was 'Home Rule All Round', with legislatures in each of the UK's four countries in charge of domestic matters.

In trying to win people over, the Scottish Home Rule Association employed the traditional campaigning methods of the time, issuing pamphlets and holding public meetings. Despite describing itself as non-partisan, it also sought to convert the Liberal Party to its cause. This made sense, as the Liberals had been the dominant party in Scotland since the 1832 Reform Act and were also the party of Home Rule in Ireland. There is evidence that the Association achieved some success in gaining public support and winning over the Liberals. According to Naomi Lloyd-Jones, Lord Rosebery told Gladstone in 1889 that the cause 'really is stirring people', with Gladstone himself making favourable noises in several of his speeches. By 1892, 18 sitting Liberal MPs were amongst the Scottish Home Rule Association's vice-presidents, with another as president.

The executive of the Scottish Liberal Association was less keen on Home Rule than the rank and file. The relationship between the Scottish Home Rule Association and the Scottish Liberal Association deteriorated through the 1890s, though the former continued to publish manifestos and try to influence MPs until 1908, when it fell into abeyance.

The Liberal Party and the Government of Scotland Bill

In the period up until the First World War, responsibility for the cause of Scottish Home Rule passed to other groups – such as the Scottish Liberal Association, Convention of the Royal Burghs of Scotland, Highland Land League, Scottish Labour League, Scottish Liberal Women's Association and the Young Scots' Society – which continued to put pressure on the Liberal Party and its MPs to introduce legislation. Unlike in Ireland, there was never any threat of civil unrest in support of Scottish Home Rule, meaning the issue remained a constitutional one to be decided in Parliament.

As Nathan Kane has described, the focus on Scottish Home Rule in Parliament prior to the First World War was largely concentrated into the years 1889–1895 and 1910–1914. It is no coincidence that these were the two periods when Irish Home Rule dominated debate, with the earlier period coming either side of Gladstone's Second Irish Home Rule Bill, and the later period being when the threat of civil war in Ulster made the issue of vital importance. Furthermore, by the later period, the veto of the House of Lords had been removed, making the passing of Home Rule legislation more likely.

Kane has argued that Scottish Home Rule was used as a way of making Irish Home Rule more palatable. Whether or not this is true, there were 13 motions in favour of Scottish Home Rule debated in Parliament between 1889 and 1924. The first of these came in April 1889 and proposed: 'That, in the opinion of this House, it is desirable that arrangements be made for giving to the people of Scotland, by their representatives in a National Parliament, the management and control of Scottish affairs.' The motion was put forward by Dr Gavin Clarke, one of five MPs for the Crofters' Party, an independent Liberal Party that wanted to change crofting laws in Scotland. Gladstone, who at the time represented Midlothian, spoke on the motion, but it was felt to be an ill-considered proposal and failed to pass.

Over time, support for Home Rule increased amongst Scottish MPs, ultimately leading in 1913 to the Government of Scotland Bill being put forward by Sir William Henry Cowan, Liberal MP for Aberdeenshire East. In introducing his bill, Cowan is reported by Kane to have addressed the claim that Home Rule did not have popular support in Scotland, stating:

> The Scottish Liberal Members to a man are declared and convinced Home Rulers. That seems rather curious if there is no demand for Home Rule in Scotland. It is well-known that ours is a cautious race, and I am perfectly certain that Scottish Members would never be so foolish as to place themselves far ahead of public opinion in Scotland upon so vital a matter as this.

The Government of Scotland Bill sought to create a Scottish Parliament along the lines of that proposed for the Irish Parliament, which would have authority over pensions, national insurance, labour exchanges and other purely Scottish affairs. However, significant powers would have remained with the then Imperial Parliament, such as war, foreign affairs, national defence, immigration, trademarks, the postal service, external trade and tax collection.

The bill passed its second reading, but was overtaken by the outbreak of the First World War in 1914, then the Easter Rising in 1916 and the subsequent war for independence in Ireland. As a result, Scottish Home Rule was forced to take a back seat.

3
Post-First World War to the Establishment of the Scottish Parliament

John MacCormick and the Birth of the Scottish National Party

In the aftermath of the First World War, several organisations tried to revive the cause of Scottish Home Rule. By this point there was a mixing of views and merging of organisations among supporters of Home Rule and independence, influenced in part by events surrounding independence in Ireland.

A second Scottish Home Rule Association was formed after the war by, amongst others, Roland Muirhead and Tom Johnston. Muirhead was described by Johnston, who later became Churchill's Secretary of State for Scotland, as the grand old man of Scottish nationalism. He was one of a group who, around 1900, formed the Young Scots League, which sought Home Rule through the Liberal Party, following which he turned to the Independent Labour Party. Johnston is quoted in the *Herald* newspaper as providing, in 1951, the following remarkable account of Muirhead's early life:

> Half a century ago he packed his bag and walked out of the family tannery business in Renfrewshire to live the free life, first in a Owenite colony in the state of Washington (USA) and then in a non-violent anarchist colony in the same state.
>
> I never rightly got the hang of what happened during his brief sojourn in these oases in the wicked world, but he was soon back in London organising a co-operative tannery and shortly thereafter he was engaged managing the old family business in Renfrewshire, which – lest you think he is simply a starry-eyed dreamer! – he has managed for years and still does with conspicuous success.

The second Scottish Home Rule Association sought to influence both the Liberal Party and, in particular, the Labour Party, which had been committed to Home Rule since its formation. As the 1920s wore on, however, the Association was superseded by other organisations, with Muirhead moving more towards full independence and going on to become involved with the National Party of Scotland and then the SNP.

Another organisation at the time was the Scots National League – an independence movement formed in London in 1921 by Ruaraidh Erskine of Mar and William Gillies. It emerged out of the Highland Land League and was part of the Gaelic tradition of self-determination, arguing for full independence rather than Home Rule. The League began contesting elections with the objective of securing a majority of Scottish MPs who were willing to withdraw from Westminster and set up an independent Scottish Parliament in Edinburgh.

The key figure in the revival of interest promoting Home Rule rather than independence during this period was John MacCormick. A remarkable figure, MacCormick is described by journalist Kenneth Roy as being, for a time, 'the most influential Scotsman alive; and one of the most celebrated'. Furthermore, Roy goes on to say that at MacCormick's funeral service, following his tragically early death at the age of 56, his friend Professor Dewar Gibb – who had been leader of the SNP – said that he 'had sacrificed worldly advancement, wealth and high position in giving himself unstintingly to Scotland'.

MacCormick was born in 1904 in Pollokshields, to a sea captain father and a mother who was the first Queen's district nurse in the Western Isles. He attended Woodside School and from there went to Glasgow University, where he graduated in arts and law. At university he became active in student politics, becoming a member of the Labour club. His real passion, though, was for greater self-government for Scotland and, together with other members of the Labour Party, he set up the Glasgow University Scottish Nationalist Association in 1927 to argue for Home Rule. He was, apparently, a fervent and eloquent advocate of the cause. Kenneth Roy recounts how MacCormick, when setting out the case for Home Rule with his usual fervour, was heckled by a member of the audience who wanted to know if Scotland would have its own 'King John' when it gained independence. The nickname stuck.

However, MacCormick didn't just make passionate speeches in favour of Home Rule, he actively sought to bring it about. Crucial to achieving greater autonomy was the need for a new political party, without links to existing parties. In 1928, MacCormick was instrumental in bringing together the Scots National League, the Scots National Movement, the Scottish

Home Rule Association, and his own organisation – the Glasgow University Scottish Nationalist Association – to form the National Party of Scotland. Reflecting the outlook of the groups that formed it, the new party was broadly centre-left in its political outlook. However, it contained people with differing views about Scotland's constitutional future, with some favouring independence and others Home Rule. Recognising that too radical an approach was stalling the party's progress, MacCormick was successful in moving it towards a more moderate position in favour of Home Rule.

In 1932, the rival Scottish Party was established by former members of the Unionist Party, its primary difference being that it took a centre-right perspective and had a different attitude towards the British Empire. However, MacCormick recognised that there was insufficient room for two parties arguing for greater Scottish autonomy and so, as Secretary of the National Party of Scotland, sought to negotiate a merger. This was agreed, and in 1934 the Scottish National Party (SNP) was born.

In 1942, however, MacCormick resigned from the SNP due to its support for independence rather than Home Rule, and – following the Second World War and together with other former SNP members – established the Scottish Convention, an idea he had first put forward in 1939. The purpose of the Scottish Convention was to bring together a cross-section of society and different shades of political opinion into an assembly, in order to demonstrate support for Home Rule and influence the main political parties. In 1949, it produced the Scottish Covenant:

We, the people of Scotland who subscribe to this Engagement, declare our belief that reform in the constitution of our country is necessary to secure good government in accordance with our Scottish traditions and to promote the spiritual and economic welfare of our nation.

We affirm that the desire for such reform is both deep and widespread through the whole community, transcending all political differences and sectional interests, and we undertake to continue united in purpose for its achievement.

With that end in view we solemnly enter into this Covenant whereby we pledge ourselves, in all loyalty to the Crown and within the framework of the United Kingdom, to do everything in our power to secure for Scotland a Parliament with adequate legislative authority in Scottish affairs.

The Scottish Covenant Association was established in 1951 to campaign for a devolved Scottish Assembly. Kenneth Roy describes this as 'a phenomenon, the like of which we had never seen before and have not seen since – a highly organised, systematic campaign to win the support of the Scottish people for a parliament in Edinburgh'. Within six months, the campaign had gained the support of a million people, with the Covenant eventually estimated to have been signed by over 2 million people – two-thirds of the Scottish electorate. Despite this, MacCormick's idea that the campaign should transcend party politics was both a strength and a weakness. Though it enabled the campaign to gain broad support, it was too easily dismissed as a pressure group and failed to attract the support of established politicians. Thus, it had little political impact at the time.

John MacCormick himself became a Liberal towards the end of the 1940s, standing unsuccessfully for Parliament several times. His sad death in 1961 meant he missed the upsurge in support for the SNP and the subsequent progress towards a Scottish Parliament, with his youngest son Neil stating that his father believed his efforts had been in vain. However, as Dewar Gibb said at his funeral: 'If in time to come a new and different Scotland comes to be erected, the work of John MacCormick will be on the headstone in the corner.'

The Rise of the SNP and the First Devolution Referendum

The SNP did not win its first parliamentary seat until 1945, when Robert McIntyre – regarded as the father of the party – won the Motherwell by-election (although he lost the seat at the general election three months later). He later qualified as a physician at Edinburgh University and became consultant chest physician for Stirlingshire and Clackmannan from 1951 until 1979.

McIntyre played a crucial role in establishing and building up the SNP in the 1940s, 50s and 60s, standing in every general election between 1945 and 1974, as well as a by-election in 1971. In her obituary of McIntyre, Winnie Ewing describes how he was accused in the press of refusing to take the oath of allegiance to the Crown. In fact, he could not find the requisite two sponsors and so walked to the Speaker's chair on his own, at which point the Speaker refused to recognise him. As this reflected badly on the House of Commons, two sponsors did finally emerge. In her obituary, Ewing quotes a moving speech given by McIntyre to a room full of SNP candidates, in which he declares: 'Once I had to use all the arts of persuasion to find one man or woman to stand so that I would not be our only candidate. Now when I look around this room, for the first time I know in my heart we shall win Scotland free.'

The slow progress made by the SNP in the post-war years is demonstrated by Table I below:

Table 1. The SNP's performance in general elections, 1945–1979

	Candidates	Seats	% Vote
1945	8	0	1.2
1950	3	0	0.4
1951	2	0	0.3
1955	2	0	0.5
1959	5	0	0.8
1964	15	0	2.4
1966	23	0	5.0
1970	65	1	11.4
1974 (Feb.)	70	7	21.9
1974 (Oct.)	71	11	30.4
1979	71	2	17.3

Source: Ian McAllister, 'Party Organisation and Minority Nationalism: A Comparative Study in the United Kingdom', European Journal of Political Research *9 (1981), p. 244.*

The rise in support for the SNP can be traced back to the early 1960s, including the 1962 West Lothian by-election where the party came a strong second. However, the real turning point came when Winnie Ewing won the 1967 Hamilton by-election with 46 per cent of the vote, with the Labour vote dropping from 71 per cent of the vote at the 1966 general election to 41.5 per cent at the by-election. Remarkably, Ewing was the first SNP MP to be elected since Robert McIntyre in 1945, and swiftly became one of the great heroes of the nationalist movement. In a 2018 BBC article, Scotland's First Minister, Nicola Sturgeon, paid tribute to Ewing as her personal political hero: 'She was somebody who changed the course of Scottish political history … and who helped define the Scottish independence movement as the outward-looking, inclusive one that we are today.'

Ewing was born Winifred Margaret Woodburn in Glasgow in 1929, the daughter of a successful small businessman, and became involved with the SNP while at Glasgow University studying law. Her victory in Hamilton was followed by a train journey down to London with 250 supporters in a train emblazoned with the SNP logo. She then proceeded to drive to Westminster in a Scottish-built Hillman Imp, where she was greeted by a large crowd and a pipe band. She famously told the press at the time: 'Stop the world, Scotland wants to get on.'

Though she lost her Hamilton seat in 1970, Ewing went on to win the Moray and Nairn seat at the 1974 general election, defeating the then Scottish Secretary, Gordon Campbell. She lost this seat in 1979, but became an MEP, earning the title of 'Madame Ecosse' from French newspaper *Le Monde* for her championing of Scottish interests. In 1999, she decided not to stand for the European Parliament and instead became an MSP for the Highlands and Islands in the Scottish Parliament. As the oldest member and 'Mother of the House', she presided over the opening of the new Scottish Parliament, declaring: 'The Scottish Parliament, adjourned on the 25th day of March in the year 1707, is hereby reconvened.' She retired from the Scottish Parliament in 2003 and stood down as president of the SNP in 2005, bringing to an end an illustrious 38-year career in representative politics.

Winnie Ewing and her victory in Hamilton symbolised the rise of the SNP during that time. According to Nathalie Duclos, there were a number of factors underlying this. One of these was that the post-war period had been dominated by Labour and the Conservatives. In the 1960s, there were clear signs of dissatisfaction with the two main parties, with some commentators seeing this as part of a longer-term trend in which people no longer identified as strongly with one or other of the parties based on their social class. A second was a perceived loss of British self-confidence as a result of economic difficulties and the disintegration of the Empire. And a third was that some parts of the UK, such as Scotland and Wales, were not thought to be doing as well – particularly economically – as others.

This provided an opening for nationalist movements in Scotland and Wales. In Scotland, the SNP instituted internal reforms to its organisation, setting up constituency associations in addition to local branches and a National Assembly to discuss policy and strategy. This involved increasing membership and hiring more full-time staff, making the party a more effective campaigning entity and helping it to capitalise on the opportunities that had arisen.

The SNP performed strongly at the May 1968 local elections, winning

107 council seats and 30 per cent of the vote across Scotland. Furthermore, Plaid Cymru's victory at the 1966 Camarthen by-election, which preceded Winnie Ewing's 1967 win in Hamilton, provides further evidence of a rise in support for greater autonomy in both Scotland and Wales.

All this ensured the issue of greater Scottish self-government continued to increase in prominence, provoking a reaction from the two major parties. Edward Heath issued his 'Declaration of Perth' at the 1968 Conservative Party Conference, committing the party to some form of Scottish devolution. The following year, Harold Wilson's Labour government responded by setting up the Royal Commission on the Constitution, which was tasked with looking at various models of devolution, federalism and confederalism. However, its final report – published in 1973 and often known as the Kilbrandon Report – after Lord Kilbrandon, its chairman at the time of publication – rejected both independence and federalism, proposing instead directly elected devolved assemblies for Scotland and Wales.

The SNP's electoral success in the 1970s only served to increase interest in Scottish issues and particularly that of devolution. This SNP surge did not happen overnight, with the party losing Hamilton at the 1970 General Election and winning only one seat elsewhere (the Western Isles). Despite this, it polled 11 per cent of the vote and, for the first time, came third in Scotland, ahead of the Liberals. Disappointing local elections followed in 1971, where the party saw its vote halved compared to 1968. However, the party's trajectory changed dramatically for the better with a series of by-elections. Having done well at the September 1971 Stirling and Falkirk by-election and the March 1973 Dundee East by-election, the SNP went on to win the November 1973 Glasgow Govan by-election, with Margo MacDonald defeating Labour in one of its safest seats. This was followed by the February 1974 general election, in which the party won 7 seats and polled over 20 per cent of the vote. A few months later, in the October 1974 general election, it fared even better, winning 11 seats and over 30 per cent of the vote.

In her analysis of the dramatic increase in support for the SNP, French scholar Nathalie Duclos highlights the findings of political scientists that, during this period, there was a rise in the number of voters concerned with specifically Scottish issues and who felt that Scotland was being neglected. The SNP was well placed to capitalise on this. Duclos also highlights the SNP's focus on two key policy issues. The first of these was the party's 'It's Scotland's Oil' campaign, which claimed that revenues from the recently discovered North Sea oil were not benefiting Scotland as much as they should. While the initial rise in SNP support predates the oil campaign, there is no doubt it played a major part in increasing the number of SNP votes and MPs during the 1970s, coinciding as it did with the Arab–Israeli War in 1973 and a quadrupling of the price of oil. It also gave the SNP a credible answer as to how an independent Scotland might be able to prosper. While this did not lead to a major increase in support for Scottish independence, with most people in Scotland remaining opposed, it did make the SNP a more credible alternative and so increased support for the party.

The other key policy issue on which the SNP focused was devolution. The party had, since its early years, sought independence as its primary aim. It now moved to support devolution as a step on the road towards this. Many party members felt unable to support something that fell well short of independence and which, indeed, was intended to prevent it. However, Duclos refers to an election study showing that the SNP's support for devolution was crucial to their performance at the 1974 general elections, and in the following years. Devolution was seen by many as a possible solution to Scotland's economic problems – therefore, the SNP being perceived as the party of devolution was a key factor in its success.

The response of the Labour government to this mid-1970s upsurge in SNP support was to introduce legislation for a devolved Scottish Assembly. Though some saw this as merely a ploy to see off the SNP, there had long been plenty of wholehearted supporters of Scottish devolution within the ranks of the Scottish Labour Party, as well as some in the Conservative Party (such as Alick Buchanan-Smith and Malcolm Rifkind, both of whom resigned as members of Margaret Thatcher's Shadow Cabinet over the issue). Prominent amongst Labour supporters of devolution was John Mackintosh, MP for Berwick and East Lothian, who in 1976 was quoted as saying in the Commons: 'People in Scotland want a degree of government for themselves. It is not beyond the wit of man to devise the institutions to meet these demands.'

Following a series of by-election defeats, James Callaghan's Labour government lost its majority, and so agreed a deal with the Scottish and Welsh nationalists whereby it would introduce legislation devolving political powers to Scotland and Wales in return for their support in Commons votes. The Scotland and Wales Bill was introduced in November 1976, but was delayed in Parliament and had to be withdrawn in February 1977. The government tried again in November 1977, this time introducing separate bills for Scotland and Wales. This led to the Scotland Act 1978, which passed with Liberal support and proposed an assembly with legislative powers in defined areas, elected on a first-past-the-post basis. Areas of responsibility included education, environment, health, home affairs, legal matters, and social services. Responsibility for agriculture, fisheries and food would be divided between the Assembly and the UK government, while the latter would retain control of electricity supply.

The Scotland Act also provided for a post-legislative referendum to approve the act. However, an amendment by Labour MP George Cunningham meant the act had to be approved by 40 per cent of the registered electorate, rather than a simple majority of those who voted. In the end, 51.6 per cent of those who voted in the 1979 referendum favoured a devolved assembly, but this represented only 33 per cent of the total electorate. As this did not meet the terms of the act, it was subsequently repealed.

The failure to deliver a Scottish Assembly proved a major setback for the SNP, with the 1979 general election seeing its share of the vote cut almost in half. Nathalie Duclos puts this down to the SNP being regarded as a busted flush due to its status as the party most associated with devolution. The salience of oil as an issue also diminished, and the whole period exposed internal divisions within the party. One split that had been apparent for some time was that between gradualists, who believed in achieving independence in stages, and fundamentalists, who believed in nothing less than full independence and saw devolution as a trap. There was also a split between traditionalists, who took a non-ideological view, and those who were more left wing and felt the party needed to attract working-class Labour voters. The parliamentary party was dominated by traditionalists, while the party's National Executive was dominated by the left, stoking internal friction. All of this meant that the SNP's influence on the constitutional debate was, for the time being, diminished.

The Second Devolution Referendum

The aftermath of the 1979 referendum saw a new Conservative government led by Margaret Thatcher. At the time of the referendum, Lord Home – a supporter of devolution – claimed there were a number of flaws in Labour's legislation, one of which was that the proposed Assembly would have no power to raise revenue, and that the Conservatives would come up with a better scheme. However, the official government position hardened against devolution during the 1980s, though there were still individual Conservatives who supported the idea, such as Michael Fry, Struan Stevenson and Brian Meek.

In opposition to the Conservative government, a new body was established – made up mainly of Labour and SNP members – to assume leadership of the movement in favour of devolution. This was the Campaign for a Scottish Assembly (CSA), set up in 1980 with Dr Jack Brand as its first chairman. Brand was an SNP member keen to ensure that Labour did not abandon its commitment to Scottish devolution following the referendum. The CSA kept the flame of Home Rule burning in the early 1980s, setting up the committee under Sir Robert Grieve that, in 1988, produced the Claim of Right for Scotland. This drew inspiration from the Declaration of Arbroath and stated:

> We, gathered as the Scottish Constitutional Convention, do hereby acknowledge the sovereign right of the Scottish people to determine the form of government best suited to their needs, and do hereby declare and pledge that in all our actions and deliberations their interests shall be paramount.
>
> We further declare and pledge that our actions and deliberations shall be directed to the following ends:
>
> To agree a scheme for an Assembly or Parliament for Scotland;
>
> To mobilise Scottish opinion and ensure the approval of the Scottish people for that scheme; and,
>
> To assert the right of the Scottish people to secure implementation of that scheme.

The Claim was signed by the bulk of Scottish MPs, the exception being the Conservatives. It was then adopted at the first meeting of the Scottish Constitutional Convention, which took over from the CSA in 1989. The convener of this body was Canon Kenyon Wright who, as noted in the *Scotsman*'s obituary, had an enormous impact on the Scottish devolution movement. Born in 1932 in Paisley to a technician father with the textile company J&P Coats, Wright graduated from the University of Glasgow before going on to study theology at Cambridge University. He then travelled to India with his wife to undertake missionary work, learning Bengali in the process. He returned to the UK in 1970 with his wife and three daughters, eventually becoming the general secretary of the Scottish Council of Churches (now called Action of Churches Together in Scotland).

As a long-time campaigner for Scottish devolution, Wright was a natural choice to chair the executive committee of the Scottish Constitutional Convention, which involved him overseeing the activities of the various working groups between the convention's plenary sessions. He displayed great skill in this role, achieving consensus across the disparate groups involved. Following his death in 2017, Scotland's First Minister, Nicola Sturgeon, observed that: 'His chairmanship of the Scottish Constitutional Convention ... was testament to his strength of character, tenacity and charisma. He was able to bring together the different strands of Scottish politics and society to achieve consensus about the way ahead for Scottish devolution.'

The other key figures in the Constitutional Convention were its co-chairs David Steel and Harry Ewing, who represented the two main political parties involved. Of the two, David Steel (now Baron Steel of Aikwood) was the better known, having been leader of the Liberal Party from 1976 – following Jeremy Thorpe's resignation – until 1988. Born in Kirkcaldy in 1938, Steel introduced, as a private member's bill, the 1967 Abortion Act, which legalised abortion under certain conditions. His time as leader of the Liberals saw the party enter into a 'Lib–Lab Pact' in 1977, the formation of the SDP–Liberal Alliance in 1981 (which secured 25 per cent of the vote at the 1983 general election, though only gained 23 seats due to the first-past-the-post electoral system), and finally a formal merger of the two parties in 1988. Having stood down as leader, Steel devoted his energies to one of his greatest passions: Home Rule for Scotland. From 1989, this involved being co-chair of the Scottish Constitutional Convention and then, when he stood down from Westminster in 1997, becoming an MSP in the first Scottish Parliament. Fittingly, given his commitment to the cause, he was the Scottish Parliament's first Presiding Officer. He also went on to chair the Scottish Liberal Democrats' internal party commission looking at how the devolved settlement could be improved. Unsurprisingly, this became known as the Steel Commission and its report, published in 2006, contains many ideas relevant to the current constitutional debate.

Harry Ewing, by contrast, had a much lower profile, but was a shrewd choice as co-chair. The son of a miner in Cowdenbeath, in his *Guardian* obituary fellow Labour MP Brian Wilson describes him as personifying 'the Presbyterian tradition within the Labour Party in Scotland – an upstanding figure, church elder, slightly conservative on social issues and always in demand to deliver the Immortal Memory at a Burns Supper, which he did often and well'.

Crucially, Ewing was a Labour loyalist who didn't defect when his friend Jim Sillars formed the breakaway Scottish Labour Party. He also had a longstanding commitment to devolution, having been under-secretary for

Scotland with responsibility for devolution in the governments of Harold Wilson and Jim Callaghan. This made him a respected figure amongst Labour MPs and when he announced in 1989 that he would not stand again as an MP, this paved the way for him to take up the role of co-chair with the Scottish Constitutional Convention.

Combined, these figures managed to bring a wide range of organisations together in the Constitutional Convention, including the Labour Party, the Liberal Democrats, the Green Party, the Scottish Trades Union Congress and the Scottish Council of Development and Industry, as well as representatives of the Catholic Church and the Church of Scotland. However, this did not include the SNP. Though involved initially, the party left due to the Convention's unwillingness to discuss independence as a constitutional option.

There was no doubt that the Labour Party, as the dominant party in Scotland, were the key players in the devolution movement throughout the 1980s and early 1990s. While consensus was necessary, devolution would not have happened without Labour support. This reflected a change within the party, which had not always been totally committed to Scottish devolution. Historically, though Labour had been a party of Home Rule, it was divided on the issue. Scottish Labour MP and later Foreign Secretary Robin Cook, who later became a strong advocate of devolution, had campaigned for a 'No' vote in the 1979 referendum, considering the devolution debate to be akin to fiddling while Rome burned. At the time, according to the *Edinburgh Evening News*, he claimed: 'Increasingly, ordinary voters find the whole business totally irrelevant to the real problems which we face in the industrial and economic fields.'

While many others in the Labour Party shared similar views, there remained plenty of others committed to Scottish devolution. Prominent amongst this group were John Smith, Donald Dewar and Gordon Brown. In common with his hero James Maxton, future Prime Minister Gordon Brown was a lifelong supporter of devolution for Scotland. Brown even wrote a biography of the Red Clydesider and leader of the Independent Labour Party, who had been a passionate advocate of Scottish Home Rule. Prior to becoming an MP, Brown refused to join the cross-party 'Yes' for Scotland campaign at the 1979 referendum. Instead, he chaired the Labour Party's own campaign for a 'Yes' vote, speaking at 30 meetings over three days as the referendum drew closer, declaring, according to the *Edinburgh Evening News*: 'To be swayed now by the scaremongering and false fears peddled by the money men of the No campaign would be like scoring an own goal in the last few seconds of a big match.'

Future Labour leader John Smith was also a sincere believer in devolution. Having been responsible for piloting the devolution proposals for Scotland and Wales through Parliament in the 1970s, he regarded the creation of a Scottish Parliament as 'unfinished business'. In a *Scotsman* article marking the twentieth anniversary of Smith's death, Mike Elrick refers to his belief that people were losing faith in the democratic process because power had become too remote and centralised. Thus, argues Elrick, Smith became a convert to devolution in the 1970s not as a means of seeing off the SNP, but as a way of addressing a democratic deficit. It would bring politicians closer to people and make them more accountable for their actions. He also thought it in the interests of the UK as a whole, as it represented a key element of democratic renewal.

Donald Dewar – who had been at Glasgow University with John Smith – was another key architect of the Scottish Parliament, and the original First Minister of Scotland when it was finally established in 1999. As Shadow Scottish Secretary in the 1980s, he took Labour into the Constitutional Convention and, according to Wendy Alexander – who worked with Dewar on the Convention – he understood 'that Scots like their constitutional change to be the product of consensus between parties'. He was, therefore, willing to accept a proportional voting system despite knowing it would probably deny his party a majority. As Scottish Secretary after Labour's victory at the 1997 election, he launched the Scotland Bill with the famous words: 'There shall be a Scottish Parliament. I like that.'

He was tasked with winning the referendum in 1997, again working with other parties – notably the Liberal Democrats and the SNP – before becoming First Minister. Sadly, his term in office was cut short by his death from a brain haemorrhage in October 2000.

With the support of such key figures, it is no surprise that the Labour Party came to support devolution in the 1980s. This was reinforced by groups within the party, such as Scottish Labour Action, which wanted the party to be far more proactive in arguing for devolution. This was driven both by conviction and political circumstance. The 1980s were dominated by Margaret Thatcher's Conservative government, and despite Labour being the largest party in Scotland, it could do little to prevent the government's policies being enacted north of the border. It therefore made sense to argue for a body that would have charge of domestic Scottish issues and be elected by Scottish voters, thereby reflecting Labour's electoral strength. It was also necessary as a means to stifle any rise in support for the SNP, something that was a constant worry for Labour, particularly following Jim Sillars's victory at the Glasgow Govan by-election in 1988.

In 1995, the Constitutional Convention produced its blueprint for devolution – 'Scotland's Parliament, Scotland's Right' – with the Labour Party then including plans for a Scottish Parliament in its manifesto for the 1997 general election. Having convincingly won that election, Labour produced a white paper on Scottish devolution based on the Constitutional Convention proposals, but with additional input from civil servants and others.

Unlike in 1979, when the referendum was held after the bill had gone through Parliament, this was to be a pre-legislative referendum. The referendum asked two questions: the first on whether there should be a Scottish Parliament, and the second on whether it should have tax-varying powers. All the major political parties in Scotland, the Conservatives excepted, supported the devolution proposals.

The result was a comfortable victory for the pro-devolution campaign, with 74.3 per cent and 63.5 per cent of people voting 'Yes' to, respectively, the first and second questions. In response, the UK Parliament passed the Scotland Act 1998, which led to the establishment of the Scottish Parliament in 1999.

The major difference with the previous devolution legislation of the 1970s was that the Scotland Act set out those powers to be retained by Westminster, with the Scottish Parliament able to legislate in any areas not reserved. However, the act maintained Westminster's continued power to legislate in respect of Scotland, in order to preserve parliamentary sovereignty. The main powers reserved to Westminster under Schedule 5 of the Scotland Act 1998 were:

- Constitutional matters
- UK foreign policy (including relations with the EU)
- UK defence and national security
- The fiscal, economic and monetary system
- Trade and industry, including competition and consumer protection
- Immigration and nationality
- Railways, transport safety and regulation
- Energy (electricity, coal, gas, nuclear)
- Employment legislation
- Social security and child support
- Gambling and the National Lottery

- Data protection
- Firearms
- Ordnance survey
- Abortion, human fertilisation, embryology, genetics
- Xenotransplantation and vivisection
- Equal opportunities
- Regulation of activities in outer space

For those matters not reserved, the act gave the Scottish Parliament full legislative competence to pass both primary and subordinate legislation. The main areas devolved were as follows:

- Health
- Education
- Justice and home affairs
- Police and fire services
- Local government
- Economic development
- Tourism
- Environment
- Criminal and civil law
- Agriculture, forestry, fishing and food
- Sport and the arts
- Planning
- Social work
- National heritage
- Training
- Housing
- Some aspects of transport, including the road network, ports and harbours
- Statistics, public registers and records

A further difference from the 1970s devolution legislation was that the Scottish Parliament would be elected by proportional representation, rather than a first-past-the-post system. This translated into 129 MSPs, with 73 elected by individual constituencies and a further 56 elected from regional party lists.

The Scotland Act 1998 also gave the Scottish Parliament full control over local taxes, council tax and business rates, as well as the ability to vary the basic rate of income tax in Scotland by 3p. This was in line with the referendum vote, which approved giving the Scottish Parliament tax-varying powers.

The New Scottish Parliament and Further Constitutional Reform

The establishment of the Scottish Parliament did not end the debate about constitutional reform in Scotland. Instead, there continued to be much discussion about the powers devolved and how they were funded, with the Scotland Act leaving many important areas of policy in the hands of Westminster. Furthermore, the Scottish Executive's functions were funded almost entirely by a block grant from Westminster, with changes determined by the Barnett Formula. This formula essentially added up the costs of devolved matters in Westminster and allocated a pro rata share to Scotland based on the size of its population relative to the UK. Though the Scottish Parliament could in theory vary the basic rate of income tax by up to 3p (it was estimated that an additional 1p on the basic rate would raise £150 million in tax receipts from Scottish taxpayers), this power was never used.

The SNP, given its support for independence, naturally wished to see the Scottish Parliament gain greater powers, and was also concerned about Scotland's lack of fiscal control. This desire for further constitutional change was not, though, confined to the SNP. In particular, the problem of having a Scottish Parliament with wide-ranging spending powers but extremely limited revenue-raising ability was recognised more widely. Some of the contributions to this debate are discussed below.

The Steel Commission

The Scottish Liberal Democrats – longstanding advocates of Home Rule for Scotland within a federal United Kingdom – were the first to launch a major enquiry into how the operation of the new Scottish Parliament and its relationship with Westminster could be improved. In 2003, an internal party commission chaired by Lord Steel was set up, with its final report eventually published in March 2006. This ground-breaking piece of work – which made explicit that a genuine Home Rule settlement needed to be based on a new written constitution, rather than an Act of Parliament as was the case with devolution – was well ahead of its time. The Steel Commission's report made a range of recommendations, including:

- A more federal framework for the UK, similar to such countries as Canada and Switzerland.
- A new written constitution for the UK, which would entrench Scotland's rights within a constitutional framework rather than through an Act of Parliament.
- As a short-term option, measures to bring about a quasi-entrenchment of devolution through a review of the Scotland Act. This would include a new mechanism requiring the Scottish Parliament's consent regarding any measures that would significantly change the devolution settlement. While such a review might include changes to the Scottish Parliament's powers, this should not replace the longer-term goal of a new written constitution.
- Enshrining the principle of subsidiarity in the new written constitution, thereby recognising the status, democratic legitimacy and role of local government.
- Scotland being given exclusive competence over: the electoral system; operation of the Scottish Parliament; transport powers; medical contracts; energy policy; and the civil service. Additionally, a review would be conducted into the strong case for Scotland gaining additional powers over: betting and gaming; public and bank holidays; human rights and equalities; marine policy; and broadcasting governance.

In particular, under the heading of 'A New Fiscal Settlement for Scotland', the Steel Commission report set out substantial recommendations on the best way of financing the Scottish government and Parliament. These are reproduced below:

- A significant increase in the accountability of the Scottish Parliament and Scottish Executive, undoing the democratic deficit inherent in the current system.
- A significant increase in transparency.
- The opportunity to improve efficiency in the use and allocation of public sector resources.
- Allowing the Scottish Parliament to have its hands on the fiscal

levers necessary to influence the direction of the Scottish economy.

- The opportunity for greater innovation and for the Scottish Government to increase the tools available to it to meet its policy objectives.
- Ensuring stability in public finances during the transitional period.

Additionally, the report laid out a ten-point plan for a new system of 'fiscal federalism', reproduced below:

1. The Scottish Parliament should be given responsibility for all taxes except for those reserved to the UK.
2. The Scottish Parliament should have the ability to vary the tax rate for each of the 'devolved' taxes.
3. The Scottish Parliament should have the ability to vary the tax base for each of the 'devolved' taxes.
4. The Scottish Parliament should have the ability to abolish existing 'devolved' taxes or to introduce new taxes, subject to specific criteria and advice provided by a Finance Commission for the Nations and Regions.
5. Administration and collection of taxes should be undertaken by the Inland Revenue/federal body on behalf of Scotland.
6. Tax revenues for those 'devolved' taxes should be automatically allocated to Scotland while tax revenues for 'reserved' taxes should be automatically allocated to the UK Government.
7. The Scottish Parliament should have the power to borrow, subject to specific criteria and advice provided by the Finance Commission for the Nations and Regions within the UK system.
8. A new needs-based equalisation formula should be established to allocate grant funding across the UK, recognising the advantages to the UK of ensuring that all areas benefit from being part of the Union.
9. The new system should take current expenditure levels as the base point thereby ensuring stability of public finances for a defined period. This should include a federal safety net which would guarantee expenditure levels during the transition period.

10. The new system should also provide incentives for measures which lead to sustainable economic growth.

The Calman Commission

Having formed a minority administration following the 2007 Scottish Parliament elections, the SNP launched a public consultation on Scotland's constitutional future called the 'National Conversation'. As part of this, it published a White Paper entitled 'Choosing Scotland's Future', which set out the options, including the party's preferred option of independence. In response, through a motion passed in the Scottish Parliament on 6 December 2007, Labour, the Conservatives and the Liberal Democrats established the Commission on Scottish Devolution, chaired by Kenneth Calman. The remit of the commission was:

> To review the provisions of the Scotland Act 1998 in the light of experience and to recommend any changes to the present constitutional arrangements that would enable the Scottish Parliament to serve the people of Scotland better, improve the financial accountability of the Scottish Parliament and continue to secure the position of Scotland within the United Kingdom.

The final report of the Calman Commission, entitled 'Serving Scotland Better: Scotland and the United Kingdom in the 21st Century', was published in June 2009, with the Conservative–Liberal Democrat coalition government elected in the 2010 UK general election promising to implement its recommendations. This formed the basis of the Scotland Act 2012, the main provisions being:

- The Scottish government having the ability to raise or lower income tax by up to 10p in the pound, with any change applied across all tax bands.
- Devolving stamp duty and landfill tax to Scotland in order that they could be replaced with new taxes specific to Scotland.
- The Scottish government having borrowing powers of up to £5 billion.
- Legislative control by the Scottish government over several more issues, including limited powers relating to drink-driving limits and air weapons.

- The creation of Revenue Scotland as a tax authority responsible for devolved taxes, with HM Revenue and Customs (HMRC) continuing to collect non-devolved taxes.

Hughes Hallett/Scott Proposals

In 2010, professors Andrew Hughes Hallett and Drew Scott also produced an important report, entitled 'Scotland: A New Fiscal Settlement', arguing for a major shift in how the Scottish Parliament was financed. The main features of their proposal are reproduced below:

- Extensive fiscal autonomy is required to provide the levers needed to guide the Scottish economy and improve its performance;
- Extended fiscal autonomy is the only arrangement consistent with increasing political and economic accountability for Scottish policymakers;
- Competence to set not only all devolved tax rates, but also all aspects of those taxes (bands, base, exemptions);
- Borrowing powers are necessary to manage the economy while observing stability conditions for the UK debt level as a whole;
- Reserved powers (tax and spending) to be limited to those with no significant economic consequences locally but important for the UK as a whole, and certain policies with development or infrastructure (physical and non-physical) implications;
- Reciprocal remittance arrangements to pay for the reserved policies;
- Limited equalisation payments via a fund linked to economic capacity, not incomes;
- Addressing potential problems of tax competition, fiscal coordination and reliable debt management are a key feature of our blueprint;
- Certain institutional changes will be necessary (a fiscal policy commission, a Scottish Treasury and/or tax service, a UK policy forum/monetary fund).

Devolution Max

A more far-reaching form of proposed devolution was 'Devolution Max' (or 'Devo Max'), sometimes called 'Full Fiscal Autonomy', different forms of which have been set out over the years. Interestingly, one such scheme was put forward in 1998 by three Conservatives – Murdo Fraser, Michael Fry and Peter Smaill – in a paper entitled 'Full Fiscal Freedom'. This reflected the fact that, following the 1997 referendum, the Conservatives had moved on from their opposition to devolution, accepting the creation of the new Parliament. The focus of some in the party thus turned to how to make the Scottish Parliament work better, particularly in relation to granting it greater fiscal powers. Backing for this idea grew in the party, and in 2005 Conservative leader David Cameron announced he would not stand in the way of giving the Scottish Parliament full taxation powers if this was supported by the Scottish Conservative Party. While such support was not forthcoming at the time, the perceived need for greater Scottish fiscal autonomy has continued to gain ground within the party, as reflected in the Calman Commission and the party's proposals to the Smith Commission, discussed below.

Andrew Wilson, the SNP MSP, also suggested a form of Devolution Max before the 2001 UK general election. He was supported in this by others in the SNP, particularly in the period before full independence began to emerge as an attainable goal. Another proposal along these lines was out forward by Paul Hallwood and Ronald MacDonald in their book *The Political Economy of Financing Scottish Government*.

In essence, Devo Max would transfer responsibility for almost all spending in Scotland to the Scottish Parliament, with the exception of foreign affairs, defence and a few other areas. To fund these responsibilities, control over all taxes would be transferred to the Scottish Parliament, with an agreed amount paid to the UK Parliament to cover reserved areas of spending – a sort of reverse Barnett Formula.

Devolution Plus

Following its establishment in 2008, the independent think tank Reform Scotland published a series of reports arguing that greater powers should be devolved to the Scottish Parliament in order to increase accountability and autonomy. In doing so, it proposed a system whereby each tier of Scottish government would be responsible for raising most of what it spends. In 2011, it published 'Devolution Plus', which proposed:

- The devolution of benefits linked to policy areas – such as housing and social inclusion – that had already been devolved. This amounted to roughly half of all spending in Scotland on social protection.
- The Scottish Parliament being completely responsible for all taxes raised in Scotland, with the exception of national insurance and value-added tax (VAT), which would remain under the control of Westminster.

In February 2012, Reform Scotland launched the Devo Plus Group, run by former Liberal Democrat MSP Jeremy Purvis and chaired by myself. The group's purpose was to promote these proposals by involving politicians from the unionist political parties, in the hope that the public would be given a clearer idea of what would happen following the referendum in the event of a 'No' vote.

Devo More

Run by the Institute for Public Policy Research (IPPR) and academic Alan Trench, 'Devo More' aimed to develop a model of enhanced devolution that would meet the needs of the UK's constituent nations within a UK-wide framework. Its first report, 'Funding Devo More', was published in January 2013 and examined fiscal options for strengthening the Union. The main recommendations in the first report included the devolution of a package of further taxes, including all income tax.

A further report was published on the devolution of welfare in March 2014, while following the independence referendum in October of the same year, Alan Trench set out his thoughts on the way forward in a article entitled, 'Devo More: The Path to a Federal UK, Not Ever Looser Union'.

4
The Independence Referendum and Its Aftermath

Alex Salmond and the Referendum on Independence

It is clear that much of the above thinking on further constitutional reform was stimulated by the election of a minority SNP administration at the 2007 Scottish Parliament elections. In the previous two sessions of the Scottish Parliament (1999–2003 and 2003–2007) the administration consisted of a Labour–Liberal Democrat coalition. During this period – despite the Steel Commission's proposals, and the SNP and various economists arguing for greater fiscal powers – there had been no real prospect of anything significant changing. It is therefore worth noting the remarkable transformation in the SNP's position from 1979, when they were written off as a spent force, and 2007. While many people played a part in this transformation, few would disagree that the key figure was Alex Salmond.

The future First Minister of Scotland was born in Linlithgow in 1954, where he attended the local primary school and then Linlithgow Academy. In a 2010 *Scotsman* article, Salmond recalled standing as the SNP candidate in his primary school's mock election, though this was due to the party being the only choice left, rather than any instinctive political affiliation. He claims to have won a landslide victory as a result of offering half-day school and ice cream instead of free school milk – an early example of his gift for retail politics!

On leaving school, Salmond studied economics at St Andrews University, where he became a member of the SNP. He then joined the civil service as an assistant economist in the Department of Agriculture and Fisheries for Scotland, before becoming an economist for the Royal Bank of Scotland from 1980 to 1987. By this time, as a prominent member of the 79 Group, he had gained a reputation as a rebel and radical. The group – which included Roseanna Cunningham, Kenny MacAskill and Margo MacDonald, and was named after the year of its foundation – wanted the SNP to take a more left-wing stance in order to capitalise on working-class support for devolution in the 1979 referendum. That Salmond was attracted to this group is perhaps unsurprising given one of his formative influences was blind Welsh poet and cleric R. S. Thomas, whose work he studied at school. Thomas was a committed Welsh nationalist, but refused to join Plaid Cymru as he believed the party did not go far enough in its opposition to English rule. Indeed, Salmond reportedly quoted an essay by Thomas on Scotland, which said:

> And so we come full circle back to the crude reality, the necessity for politics, distasteful as they may appear. For it is England, the home of the industrial revolution, and the consequent 20th-century rationalism, that have been the winter on our native pastures, and we must break their grip, and the grip of all the quislings and yes-men before we can strike that authentic note.

The formation of the 79 Group coincided with a difficult period for the SNP, which lost 9 of its 11 MPs at the 1979 general election. This led to disagreement about future party strategy. Winnie Ewing, for example, did not want the party to appear ideological, so set up the Campaign for Nationalism in Scotland in order to oppose the 79 Group. In 1981, five members of the 79 Group – including Jim Sillars, who had joined the SNP in 1980 – were elected to the SNP's National Executive. The SNP, following a speech by Sillars, also adopted a policy of 'Scottish Resistance', calling for political strikes and civil disobedience. This included a plan whereby Sillars and others would break into Edinburgh's Royal High School building to read out a declaration on what they would do to counter unemployment. However, they were arrested before they could do so and shortly afterwards the minutes of a meeting of the 79 Group were leaked, revealing discussion of an invitation from Sinn Fein to speak at their conference. While Alex Salmond moved to reject the request and won, the association was damaging to the group. Following this, SNP leader Gordon Wilson was successful in banning internal political groupings within the party, and so the 79 Group – as well as Winnie Ewing's group – was disbanded. A committee named the 79 Group Socialist Society was established to form a new body outside the party, but the SNP quickly deemed membership of the committee to be incompatible with membership of the party. Thus, Alex Salmond, Kenny MacAskill and others were expelled from the SNP, though they were quickly readmitted and many went on to play leading roles in the party.

In 1987, Alex Salmond became MP for Banff and Buchan, taking the seat from the Conservatives. His rebellious streak was again in evidence when he was banned from the House of Commons for a week after interrupting the Chancellor's budget speech. This was done in protest at the introduction of the Poll Tax in Scotland and the reduction of income tax for high earners. In a remarkable turnaround, he succeeded Gordon Wilson as SNP leader in 1990, defeating Margaret Ewing. However, Jim Sillars supported Ewing, marking the start of a deterioration in his relationship with Salmond and disagreement over party strategy. As leader, Salmond adopted a more gradualist approach to independence by supporting devolution and campaigning with Labour and the Liberal Democrats in the 1997 referendum. Sillars saw this as a mistake and argued for a more fundamentalist position. This became the major fault line within the party.

Salmond's thinking also developed during his time as leader. Under his leadership, the party adopted a centre-left position, leading in the first Scottish Parliament elections to a proposed 'Penny for Scotland' policy of increasing income tax. However, he also understood the importance of wealth creation and growth, supporting a reduction in corporation tax to foster entrepreneurial activity and business expansion.

In 2000, Salmond stood down as leader of the SNP, with John Swinney taking over, but returned in 2004 following the party's disappointing 2003 Scottish Parliament election campaign. The 2007 election, however, saw a dramatic upswing in the party's fortunes, with a clever campaign focusing on the importance of sustainable economic growth leading to the SNP becoming the largest party in the Scottish Parliament.

This victory marked a major turning point for the Scottish Parliament. Although the SNP was a minority administration during the period 2007–2011, it took the opportunity to start its 'National Conversation' consultation exercise on Scotland's constitutional future. The white paper it published as part of this consultation contained a draft referendum bill outlining four possible options: 1) no change; 2) devolution as proposed by the Calman Commission; 3) further devolution; and 4) full independence. In February 2010, the Scottish government published a version of the draft referendum bill for public consultation, this time outlining three proposals: 1) the Calman proposals; 2) so-called 'Devolution Max'; and 3) full independence. The bill failed to pass in the Scottish Parliament and was withdrawn in September 2010.

The commitment to hold a referendum was repeated in the SNP manifesto for the 2011 Scottish Parliament elections. In advance of the election, Alex Salmond stated his preference for a referendum in the second half of the parliamentary term, as he wanted the Scottish Parliament to be given the new powers proposed by the Calman Commission (which became the Scotland Act 2012). The SNP won the election with an overall majority, meaning it now had the support it needed for an independence referendum within the Scottish Parliament. However, as the constitution was a reserved issue under the Scotland Act 1998, holding such a referendum required negotiations with the UK government in order to transfer the required powers.

The UK government agreed to transfer these powers under Section 30 of the Scotland Act, provided the referendum was 'fair, legal and decisive'. The main area of disagreement between the two governments was over the framing of the question itself, with Alex Salmond favouring the inclusion of a third option involving some form of extended devolution (such as Devo Max), which he hoped would be accepted if full independence was rejected. Furthermore, the Scottish government wanted wording that framed voting 'Yes' as being for independence – an important psychological point. It also wanted the vote to be extended to 16–18 year olds, as it was felt younger voters would be more likely to vote in favour of independence. Lastly, it wanted two questions: the first for independence and the second for the proposed 'third way'. Much of the preparation work was negotiated by Michael Moore, the Secretary of State for Scotland, and Nicola Sturgeon, the Deputy First Minister. The final position was then discussed between Alex Salmond and David Cameron in October 2012, with the only key point on which the latter remained intransigent being the removal of the second 'third way' question. With polls at the time showing only around 30 per cent support for independence, Cameron was confident of success and did not want a second question confusing the issue. Ultimately, this option was removed from the proposed referendum design, allowing both governments to sign the Edinburgh Agreement.

The Edinburgh Agreement allowed the Scottish Parliament to legislate for a single-question referendum on independence before the end of 2014. The wording of the question was to be decided by the Scottish Parliament, but subject to review by the Electoral Commission. The legislation passed in June 2013 and in November of the same year the Scottish government published its 'Scotland's Future' white paper, setting out the case for independence, as well as how this would come about. The date for the referendum was set for 18 September 2014, with all those aged 16 and over entitled to vote. The agreed question was: 'Should Scotland be an independent country?'

The prospect of the referendum led to all three unionist parties recognising the need for further devolution in the event of a 'No' vote. In October 2012, the Liberal Democrats published their initial Home Rule and Community Rule Commission report, which set out significant proposals for further fiscal powers. This was later followed up by another report in 2014. Although initially both reluctant, the Scottish Conservatives and Labour followed suit and set up their own commissions, which proposed going beyond the powers devolved in the Scotland Act 2012, particularly in relation to welfare and fiscal powers. However, due to the lack of agreement between the three unionist parties, there remained a lack of clarity regarding which powers would be devolved in the event of a 'No' vote. This weakness was highlighted particularly in the second of the head-to-head televised debates, where the three leaders of the Scottish parties were at odds regarding further potential constitutional changes.

Part of the reason for this lack of clarity was that for most of the referendum debate 'No' supporters were supremely confident of winning, with polls at the start of campaigning indicating a comfortable 70/30 split in their favour. The 'No' campaign's main focus was demonstrating the flaws in independence, such as the continued use of sterling in an independent Scotland and the impact on the Scottish economy. The term 'Project Fear' first came to prominence during this period, being much used by the SNP in regards to their opponents' political strategy of economic scaremongering. In fact, it is Rob Shorthouse who is credited with coining the term, apparently as a joke in an interview he gave at the time – the irony being that he was director of communications for the campaign in favour of the 'No' vote.

The complacency of the 'No' campaign dissolved abruptly in the final few weeks before the referendum, with polls indicating a sharp narrowing in support between 'Yes' and 'No'. For a time, as can be seen in the figure above, YouGov polls even indicated the 'Yes' vote had a majority (Figure 1). This galvanised the unionist parties into making explicit what the Scottish Parliament's new powers might look like in the event of a 'No' vote. This move towards greater clarity began with Gordon Brown unveiling a timetable for delivering new powers, which suggested a command paper would be published in October, and a draft bill would ready by the end of January 2015. In doing so, he commented: 'We're going to be, within a year or two, as close to a federal state as you can be in a country where one nation is 85 per cent of the population.'

This was followed up by the so-called 'vow', which appeared on the front page of the *Daily Record* on 15 September 2014, and was signed by

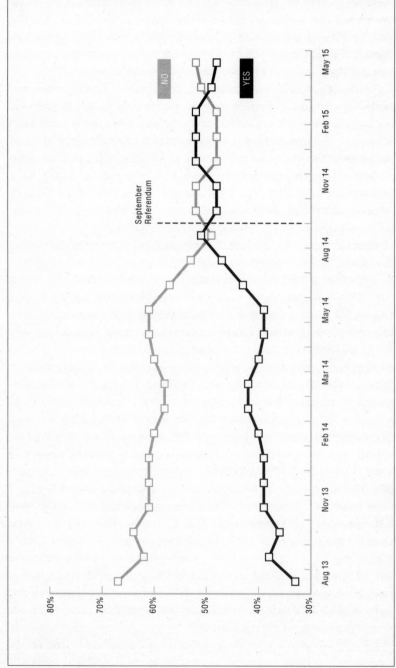

Figure I. Voting intentions in the event of a referendum on Scottish independence

David Cameron, Nick Clegg and Ed Miliband – the leaders, respectively, of the Conservatives, Liberals and Labour parties. It stated that:

> The Scottish Parliament is permanent and extensive new powers for the Parliament will be delivered by the process and to the timetable agreed and announced by our three parties, starting on 19th September.
>
> And it is our hope that the people of Scotland will be engaged directly as each party works to improve the way we are governed in the UK in the years ahead.
>
> We agree that the UK exists to ensure opportunity and security for all by sharing our resources equitably across all four nations to secure the defence, prosperity and welfare of every citizen.
>
> And because of the continuation of the Barnett allocation for resources, and the powers of the Scottish Parliament to raise revenue, we can state categorically that the final say on how much is spent on the NHS will be a matter for the Scottish Parliament.
>
> We believe that the arguments that so powerfully make the case for staying together in the UK should underpin our future as a country. We will honour those principles and values not only before the referendum but after.
>
> People want to see change. A No vote will deliver faster, safer and better change than separation.

How great a difference the vow made to the referendum result is impossible to tell. However, on 18 September 2014 Scotland voted 'No' to independence by 55.3 per cent (2 million people) to 44.7 per cent (1.6 million people), on a turnout of 84.6 per cent. The following day, Prime Minister David Cameron issued a statement in which he said:

> To those in Scotland sceptical of the constitutional promises made, let me say this: we have delivered on devolution under this government, and we will do so again in the next Parliament.
>
> The three pro-union parties have made commitments, clear commitments, on further powers for the Scottish Parliament. We will ensure that they are honoured in full.
>
> And I can announce today that Lord Smith of Kelvin – who so successfully led Glasgow's Commonwealth Games – has agreed to oversee the process to take forward the devolution commitments,

with powers over tax, spending and welfare all agreed by November and draft legislation published by January.

In response, all the main political parties in Scotland agreed to participate in the Smith Commission, with Alex Salmond stating: 'The Scottish government will contribute fully to a process to empower the Scottish Parliament and the Scottish people.'

The Smith Commission

The Smith Commission, chaired by Lord Smith of Kelvin, was asked by the UK government to: 'convene cross-party talks and facilitate an inclusive engagement process across Scotland to produce, by 30 November 2014, Heads of Agreement with recommendations for further devolution of powers to the Scottish Parliament'.

The Commission consisted of ten members, with two nominations from each of the five political parties represented in the Scottish Parliament: SNP, Labour, Conservative, Liberal Democrat and Green. Working to a tight timescale, it called for submissions from individuals and organisations by 31 October. The unionist parties – Labour, the Liberal Democrats and the Conservatives – all put in submissions that reflected the findings of the commissions they had set up prior to the referendum. The SNP Scottish government and the Scottish Green Party, which had supported a 'Yes' vote, both submitted proposals that were closer to Devolution Max.

Despite the differences between the parties' proposals, a set of recommendations was agreed upon in the report published on 27 November 2014. These came under three main Heads of Agreement:

- Pillar 1: providing a durable but responsive constitutional settlement for the governance of Scotland.
- Pillar 2: delivering prosperity, a healthy economy, jobs, and social justice.
- Pillar 3: strengthening the financial responsibility of the Scottish Parliament.

A Scottish Parliament Information Centre (SPICe) briefing on the report, the relevant parts of which are reproduced below, summarises its key recommendations:

- UK legislation will state that the Scottish Parliament and Scottish government are permanent institutions.
- The Sewel Convention, under which the UK Parliament will only legislate on devolved matters with the agreement of the Scottish Parliament, will be placed in statute.
- The Scottish Parliament will have full powers over elections to the Scottish Parliament and local government elections; the parties have called on the UK Parliament to devolve these powers in time to allow the Scottish Parliament to extend the franchise to 16 and 17-year olds for the 2016 Scottish Parliamentary elections.
- The inter-governmental machinery between the Scottish and UK governments (including the Joint Ministerial Committee) should be reformed and scaled up.
- The Scottish Parliament should have responsibility for the management of the Crown Estate's economic assets in Scotland, and the revenue generated from these assets.
- The State pension will remain reserved to Westminster, including new single-tier pension, entitlements to legacy state pensions whether in payment or deferred, pension credit and the rules on state pension age.
- Both the UK and Scottish parliaments will share control of income tax but the Scottish Parliament will have the power to set the rates of income tax and the thresholds at which these are paid for the non-savings and non-dividend income of Scottish taxpayers.
- The receipts raised in Scotland by the first 10 percentage points of the standard rate of VAT will be assigned to the Scottish government's budget.
- The power to charge tax on air passengers leaving Scottish airports will be devolved as will the power to charge tax on the commercial exploitation of aggregate in Scotland.
- The devolution of further responsibility for taxation and public spending, including elements of the welfare system, should be accompanied by an updated fiscal framework for Scotland, but the Barnett Formula should continue. The revised funding framework should result in the devolved Scottish budget benefiting in full from policy decisions by the Scottish government that increase revenues or reduce expenditure, and

the devolved Scottish budget bearing the full costs of policy decisions that reduce revenues or increase expenditure.

- Additional borrowing powers should be provided to 'ensure budgetary stability and provide safeguards to smooth Scottish public spending in the event of economic shocks'.
- Universal Credit will remain a reserved benefit administered and delivered by the Department for Work and Pensions (DWP). However, the Scottish government will have the power to change the frequency of Universal Credit payments, vary the existing plans for single household payments, and pay landlords direct for housing costs in Scotland. The Scottish Parliament will also have the power to vary the housing cost elements of Universal Credit, including varying the under-occupancy charge and local housing allowance rates, eligible rent, and deductions for non-dependents.
- Powers over the following benefits will be devolved to the Scottish Parliament:

  - Benefits for carers, disabled people and those who are ill:
    - Attendance Allowance
    - Carer's Allowance
    - Disability Living Allowance (DLA)
    - Personal Independence Payment (PIP)
    - Industrial Injuries Disablement Allowance
    - Severe Disablement Allowance

  - Benefits which currently comprise the Regulated Social Fund:
    - Cold Weather Payment
    - Funeral Payment
    - Sure Start Maternity Grant
    - Winter Fuel Payment

  - Discretionary Housing Payments

The Smith report also called for greater inter-governmental co-operation on a number of 'additional policy matters' with a view to finding ways for the Scottish Government and Parliament to exert a degree of influence over the following policy areas:

- food labelling and recognition under EU law of a 'Made in Scotland' brand
- HE students who graduate from Scotland's colleges and universities to remain in Scotland for a defined period
- the temporary right of victims of human trafficking to remain in Scotland
- the provision of certain services to Asylum seekers, including the right to lodge an asylum claim from within Scotland
- the ability of MSPs to make direct appeals to UK immigration authorities on behalf of their constituents in relation to devolved matters
- the retention by the Scottish government of fines, forfeitures, fixed penalties imposed by courts and tribunals in Scotland, as well as sums recovered under Proceeds of Crime legislation
- the potential for Scotland to have an 'opt-in' option in relation to levy-raising
- the functions and operations of the Health and Safety Executive in Scotland

The Campaign for Scottish Home Rule

During the period following the independence referendum, I set up and chaired the Campaign for Scottish Home Rule (CSHR), which involved people associated with Scotland's five main political parties, as well as others from outside traditional party politics. The group was set up in expectation of a substantial Home Rule settlement following the 'vow' made by party leaders prior to the referendum, pronouncements made by such figures as Gordon Brown, and the initial establishment of the Smith Commission.

The aim of the CSHR was to influence the Smith Commission and the ensuing legislative process, in order to bring about a Home Rule settlement that would:

- Make the Scottish Parliament genuinely accountable and democratic.
- Give the Scottish Parliament the tools required to increase prosperity and economic opportunity, tackle inequality and bring about a fairer and more sustainable society.

- Bring decision-making closer to people, thereby enabling responses to distinct Scottish priorities, opportunities and challenges.

To this end, the CSHR set out three guiding principles on which a Home Rule settlement should be based:

- **Responsibilities devolved:** A presumption in favour of devolving responsibilities to Holyrood, with a review of Schedule 5 of the Scotland Act 1998 and the burden of proof resting with Westminster should it wish to retain a responsibility.
- **Raising what you spend:** Ensure that Holyrood and Westminster have responsibility for their respective tax and borrowing powers, making each responsible for raising the money it spends.
- **Mutual respect:** Improve the relationship between parliaments and secure the permanence of the Scottish Parliament, something that would almost certainly require a written constitution or similar for the UK.

The CSHR's view of the eventual Smith Commission recommendations was that they did not meet these principles. More than this, they were not based on *any* underlying principles, and were instead the result of a political horse trade determined by the various party proposals. This meant the proposed solution was unlikely to be either sustainable or stable, as it had not been built on a consensus about the type of Home Rule settlement the people of Scotland wanted and needed.

The CSHR sought to build such a consensus through a consultation exercise conducted online and at a series of events across Scotland. However, the campaign's efforts were ignored by the UK government as it prepared the legislation that was to become the Scotland Act 2016.

Scotland Act 2016

The Scotland Act received Royal Assent and became law in March 2016. Its provisions largely implemented the recommendations of the Smith Commission, devolving significant new powers in relation to taxation and welfare (though, to date, not all of these have actually been devolved).

However, the new tax powers stopped well short of enabling the Scottish government to raise the money it spends, and the welfare powers failed to transfer responsibility for the major areas of pensions and most aspects of Universal Credit.

The act also transferred control of Scottish Parliament elections to Holyrood and put the Sewel Convention – whereby Westminster would not normally legislate on devolved matters without the consent of the Scottish Parliament – in statutory form. Furthermore, the act sought to ensure the permanence of the Scottish Parliament as an institution by stating that it could only be abolished following a referendum in Scotland. However, there is significant disagreement as to how strong this statutory mechanism is, with Dr Mike Gordon, for example, in a blog piece for the Scottish Constitutional Futures Forum, accusing the UK government of 'failing to offer something which has the appearance of the strong statutory commitment which might have been created'.

Brexit and Calls for a Second Independence Referendum

Alex Salmond, having resigned as leader of the SNP the day after the referendum result was announced, was succeeded by his deputy, Nicola Sturgeon. Born in Irvine in 1970, Sturgeon became an SNP member at the age of 16 due to her feeling that it was wrong for Scotland to be governed by a Tory government – led by Margaret Thatcher – that it hadn't elected. According to a BBC profile, Sturgeon was attracted to the SNP rather than the more obvious choice of Labour as she was 'persuaded by the argument that the nation would only truly prosper with independence'.

Having studied law at Glasgow University, Sturgeon worked as a solicitor before becoming an MSP in 1999 at the age of 29. She had intended to run for the leadership in 2004, until Alex Salmond approached her to run on a joint ticket. After some thought, she accepted his offer. Initially, with Alex Salmond still an MP in Westminster, Sturgeon acted as the SNP's leader at Holyrood, her performances in the Scottish Parliament serving to raise her profile. The SNP's historic victory in the 2007 Scottish Parliament election also saw her win the seat of Glasgow Govan, won by Margo MacDonald and Jim Sillars for the SNP in famous by-elections of the past. Sturgeon demonstrated her competence as a minister when holding the tricky health brief and, after the SNP gained an outright majority in 2011, she was given the role of overseeing the independence referendum.

Following the disappointment of the referendum, Sturgeon got down to work as First Minister and was rewarded with the SNP's incredible 2015 General Election result, when it won 56 of 59 Scottish seats. At the UK level, however, the Conservatives gained an overall majority, leading Prime Minister David Cameron to call a referendum on whether the UK should remain in the EU. A month before the referendum was due to take place in June 2016, the SNP again performed strongly in Scottish Parliament elections, comfortably emerging as the largest party. Despite this, it failed to do as well as it had in 2011, dropping from 69 seats to 63 and losing its overall majority in the process. Meanwhile, the Scottish Conservatives, led by Ruth Davidson, made big gains, leapfrogging Labour to become the second-largest party in the Scottish Parliament. Then came the Brexit referendum, which changed the political landscape dramatically. While the UK as a whole voted 52 per cent to 48 per cent in favour of leaving the EU, Scotland voted 62 per cent to 38 per cent in favour of remaining, with every council area in Scotland voting to remain. The SNP's manifesto for the Scottish Parliament elections had stated: 'The Scottish Parliament should have the right to hold another referendum … if there is a significant and material change in the circumstances that prevailed in 2014, such as Scotland being taken out the EU against our will.'

On 24 June, the day after the Brexit referendum, Nicola Sturgeon announced that the option of another independence referendum should be put on the table. Following much discussion within her party and pressure from activists, Sturgeon announced in March 2017 that she was asking the Scottish Parliament to formally request a Section 30 order – necessary for a legally binding referendum on independence to be held – from Westminster. This was turned down by then Prime Minister Theresa May, who responded that 'Now is not the time' for another referendum. Instead, she called a general election for 8 June 2017, at which the nature of Nicola Sturgeon's gamble became apparent. Opposition to another independence poll, which many felt had been divisive, was compounded by a sense of voter fatigue following successive referendums and elections in Scotland. The general election's Scottish results were, therefore, disappointing for the SNP, which lost 21 seats, with the Conservatives gaining 12, Labour 6 and the Liberal Democrats 3. Although the SNP still had 35 seats in Westminster, Sturgeon conceded that plans for another referendum had been a factor in the result and promised to reflect accordingly. Her opponents, meanwhile, called on the plans to be dropped altogether.

This did not happen, and in April 2019 Sturgeon announced that the people of Scotland should have the opportunity to make a decision on the country's future before the next Scottish Parliament elections in 2021, but after Brexit had been determined. The Scottish government also introduced the Referendums (Scotland) Bill in May 2019, providing the basis for holding a second independence referendum should it be empowered to do so by Westminster. By this time, the Conservative government at Westminster was in turmoil over Brexit, the initial date set for the UK leaving the EU having passed. The Conservatives' position was further exacerbated by disastrous European election results and the emergence of Nigel Farage's Brexit Party.

In Scotland, the European election results saw the SNP gain nearly 40 per cent of the vote, while in the UK as a whole the elections precipitated the resignation of Theresa May. None of the prospective candidates for the Conservative leadership offered to grant Nicola Sturgeon another independence referendum, with the eventual winner and current Prime Minister Boris Johnson having made no moves in this direction since his victory. By contrast, the then Labour leader Jeremy Corbyn indicated he would be willing to consider such a referendum in the future, much to the consternation of the leader of the Scottish Labour party, Richard Leonard. The result of the 12 December 2019 general election, which saw the return of the Conservative government with a comfortable majority, means that there is no immediate prospect of another independence referendum. This is despite the strong performance of the SNP in the election, in which it won 48 seats (a gain of 13), with 45 per cent of the Scottish vote. The Conservatives have since made it clear that they expect the Scottish government to abide by its pledge during the referendum campaign that this would be a once-in-a-generation event. The SNP counter this argument by asserting that Scotland being taken out of the EU despite 62 per cent of people in Scotland voting to remain has created the circumstances justifying another referendum. The period leading up to the next Scottish Parliament elections in May 2021 will now be critical, with the UK having now formally left the EU and negotiations on a trade deal underway. The waters have also been muddied by Alex Salmond's trial for sexual offences, at which he was acquitted of all charges, and its continuing ramifications for the SNP. Much will depend on the result of the Scottish elections in May 2021 and whether the SNP, with or without support from the Greens, can win a majority on a manifesto pledge to hold a referendum.

For over a hundred years, two distinct philosophical debates have driven Scottish constitutional change: Scottish nationalism vs United Kingdom nationalism, and centralists vs de-centralists. Their histories have inter-twined as different philosophies have ebbed and flowed to drive the direction of change. The last decade of debate on constitutional change around the referendum has been far more focused on the nationalist philosophy – it is now time to redress this imbalance.

Devolution, Home Rule and federalism are all at their core about de-centralisation, their supporters coming from all the parties in Scotland. In a two-question referendum, both philosophies are addressed. The country can decide in the first question on whether they want full sovereignty for Scotland, while the second question would determine whether the Scottish people want Home Rule, with much more decentralisation and shared sovereignty. If the Scottish public vote for neither of these, then they are accepting full UK sovereignty and with it a still largely centralised form of government. The next section looks at what that second choice for Home Rule might look like.

PART 2
THE STRUCTURE OF SCOTTISH HOME RULE

5
What Is Home Rule?

As has already been discussed, the concept of Home Rule is not always clearly understood and has often been misrepresented. This has sometimes been deliberate and at other times inadvertent. What it does demonstrate, though, is the idea's potency, which in turn explains the desire of groups and individuals to package their preferred set of constitutional proposals under this label. In reality, Home Rule is distinct from both independence and current devolved government, and it is important this is more widely appreciated. Only then will we be able to have a fully informed debate on the constitutional options available to Scotland, as well as to the UK as a whole.

The distinction between Home Rule and independence is apparent from the history of the various campaigns for greater Scottish self-government. Essentially, the supporters of Home Rule and independence had, and continue to have, very different goals. From its inception, the Scottish Home Rule Association made clear that it did not seek to end the Union, but instead wanted control over domestic affairs to be exercised in Scotland. Meanwhile, Westminster – or what at that time was called the Imperial Parliament – would have responsibility for controlling matters related to governance of the Empire, such as foreign affairs, defence and external trade. This desire for purely Scottish issues to be transferred to a Scottish Parliament was reflected in the 1914 Government of Scotland Bill, which fell due to the outbreak of the First World War. Largely speaking, those who wished to end altogether the Union between Scotland and the rest of the United Kingdom initially worked with the supporters of Home Rule. This no doubt stemmed from a pragmatic recognition that full independence was unachievable at the time, with Home Rule representing a potential step along the road towards this aim. It was only in the 1920s that prominent groups and individuals started to argue for full independence more explicitly. In the period leading up to the formation of the Scottish National Party in 1934, there was still an alliance – uneasy though it may have been at times – between those arguing for Home Rule and those arguing for full independence. However, in 1942 a formal breach occurred when John MacCormick left the SNP over its support for independence rather than Home Rule. From that point on, the two movements have been clearly separate, with very different end goals.

This has not prevented their interests from coming into alignment at times, as it was the increase in support for the SNP in the 1960s and 1970s that led to renewed interest in a devolved Scottish Assembly or Parliament. Nor has it stopped the two movements from working together at times, in particular during the devolution referendum campaigns of 1979 and 1997. The SNP's support for devolution was not without controversy within the party, with many regarding it as a trap standing in the way of full independence. This difference in approach between those who advocate achieving independence in stages and those who wish to achieve it in one fell swoop, often characterised as gradualists versus fundamentalists, has been evident within the SNP for many years. It remained apparent even after the Scottish Parliament was established, in the form of arguments about whether there should be a third option in the 2014 independence referendum – as favoured by Alex Salmond – or whether this would simply reduce support for full independence. However, this internal SNP debate has ultimately only ever been about how best to achieve full independence, which represents a very different goal to Home Rule.

The distinction between Home Rule and the current devolved settlement is less obvious, as both involve a division of powers between the Scottish and UK tiers of government. The history of the Home Rule movement has done little to clarify this distinction, with the terms 'Home Rule' and 'devolution' often used interchangeably by the various groupings arguing for greater self-government. However, Home Rule *is* different from devolution, as the late distinguished economist Sir Donald MacKay explained in the 2011 Reform Scotland publication, 'Scotland's Economic Future':

> Devolved government is not home rule government. Under devolution, powers are handed down by ordinary legislation of the Westminster Parliament and can be changed by ordinary legislation. Hence, the commonly expressed view that 'power devolved is power retained'. However, historically, Home Rule was seen as a structure which defined the federal area of competence and left the rest to state or provincial parliaments – the home countries being the evident British equivalent. Within a federal system, it is common practice

to entrench the powers of the states or the provinces which means that they can only be changed with the prior consent of the latter. That is, at each of the two levels the parliaments or legislatures were sovereign or independent in their defined fields of competence.

It is this concept of sovereignty being split between the UK and Scottish parliaments that fundamentally differentiates Home Rule from both independence and devolution. With independence, sovereignty rests exclusively with the Scottish Parliament, while in the current devolved context sovereignty ultimately rests with the UK Parliament at Westminster. Regarding the split sovereignty demanded by Home Rule, it is key that a written constitution exists to underpin it – a point emphasised by the Steel Commission. Systems of split sovereignty exist in many countries around the world today, examples being the United States, Canada, Switzerland, Germany and Australia. It is the constitutional arrangements used in these countries that should be emulated in any Home Rule settlement for Scotland, as they represent the best way of meeting the needs of both Scotland and the UK.

6
Home Rule in the Modern World

It is important to give people a clear idea of what a genuine Home Rule settlement for Scotland would look like and how it might be brought about. Above all, a Home Rule settlement is only workable if there is widespread acceptance that some functions are better carried out at the UK level and some are at the Scottish level. Following the debates over devolution that led to the establishment of the Scottish Parliament in 1999, there is broad consensus that some powers are better devolved to the Scottish Parliament, with no party or group seriously advocating its abolition. The devolved settlement, as originally set out in the 1998 Scotland Act, also set out which responsibilities should remain at a UK level and therefore be reserved to Westminster. However, these arrangements have since evolved, with the act being significantly amended on two subsequent occasions and further powers devolved to the Scottish Parliament. Moreover, a rise in support for the SNP and independence – as demonstrated by recent elections and the 2014 independence referendum result – provides further evidence that there is, as yet, no clear consensus on the respective powers of the UK and Scottish parliaments.

Reaching such a consensus will, ultimately, require people in Scotland to choose between the status quo, a Home Rule settlement, and independence. If independence is chosen then the answer to which powers should be exercised at the UK level is clear: none. If the status quo is maintained then full sovereignty remains with the UK. If, however, Home Rule is chosen, then UK-wide decisions must be accepted by Scots in areas that remain UK responsibilities, while the UK must recognise that Scottish responsibilities have been fully transferred to Scotland. In areas where Scottish and UK responsibilities overlap, there should be discussion between the two governments – though ultimately in such cases the final decision must rest with the UK government. Therefore, for Home Rule to work to its full potential, what is required is a crystal-clear statement of which powers will be the responsibility of the UK Parliament and which will be devolved to the Scottish Parliament. The starting point for a Home Rule settlement for Scotland thus involves defining the competence of the UK government, with all remaining functions left to the Scottish Parliament. This is the concept of 'reserved matters', described by David Torrance in a House of Commons briefing paper as: 'Political powers – legislative or executive – that are held exclusively by a particular political authority, usually in multi-national states such as the United Kingdom of Great Britain and Northern Ireland, or in federal countries such as the United States of America, Canada and Australia.'

It should be pointed out that Canada's approach to defining the respective responsibilities of the two levels of government is the other way round from that proposed for Scottish Home Rule, with the country's constitution setting out the powers of its provincial and territorial (rather than national) governments and leaving the rest to the federal government. However, the principle of reserved UK powers underpins the Scotland Act 1998 (as well as devolution to Northern Ireland and Wales), with all powers not specifically reserved in the act considered devolved to Scotland. It is, therefore, familiar and easily understood, as well as fully in keeping with the principle of subsidiarity. For these reasons, it is the approach adopted here.

7
The Division of Powers

Within the system of Home Rule outlined in this book, the functions exercised at the UK level are, though extremely important, relatively few in number. In deciding on where powers should lie, the Campaign for Scottish Home Rule (CSHR) argued that there should be a presumption in favour of devolving power to the Scottish Parliament. This principle of subsidiarity does not mean every power should be devolved, but rather that the burden of proof lies with Westminster to explain why a particular function should be exercised at the UK level.

This principle is a good guide and can be applied to the division of powers set out in Schedule 5 of the Scotland Act 1998 (as amended in 2012 and 2016). The Scotland Act divided reserved matters into two categories: general reservations and specific reservations. Under the Home Rule settlement set out in this book, the general reservations would for the most part continue to be carried out at the UK level. However, within them are some areas that, on the basis of subsidiarity, would be passed to the Scottish government level. It should be emphasised, however, that the division of powers set out below is not inherent to any Home Rule settlement. Rather, it is a judgement call and a matter for debate.

General Reservations

The current general reservations are numbered below. For each, a suggestion is given in parentheses – either for the general reservation in its entirety, or for particular areas within it – as to whether the powers should lie with the UK or Scotland.

1. Certain Aspects of the Constitution (including the Crown, the Union, the UK Parliament, the existence of the (criminal) High Court of Justiciary and the existence of the (civil) Court of Session)

- **The Crown, the UK Parliament and the Union (UK)**
  In any Home Rule settlement, certain aspects of the constitution, such as the Crown, the UK Parliament and the Union, would continue to be reserved matters. However, though ultimate responsibility for the Union should rest at the UK level, the current basis of this relationship must change, with the powers of the UK and Scottish parliaments constitutionally entrenched and any changes to this settlement requiring the agreement of both parties.

- **High Court of Justiciary and Court of Session (Scotland)**
  Given that Scots law and the Scottish justice system have always been regarded as distinctive areas that should be devolved, there is no obvious reason why the existence of the High Court of Justiciary and Court of Session in Scotland should be reserved matters. Therefore, responsibility should be transferred to Scotland.

2. The Registration and Funding of Political Parties

- **UK political parties (UK)**
  The UK Parliament would continue to be a reserved matter in a Home Rule settlement, meaning the registration and funding of political parties standing for election to the UK Parliament would also remain a reserved matter.

- **Scottish political parties (Scotland)**
  There is no reason why this power should not be exercised at the Scottish level for parties that are only standing for the Scottish Parliament or in Scotland's local elections. Thus, under a Home Rule settlement, matters relating to the registration and funding of purely Scottish political parties would be a Scottish responsibility.

3. International Relations (including with territories outside the UK and the European Union, international development and the regulation of international trade) (UK)

The proposals for both Irish and Scottish Home Rule in the 19th and early 20th centuries reveal a clear precedent for this area of policy being the responsibility of the UK government. In those cases, a distinction was drawn between domestic affairs – which were to be the domain of Home Rule parliaments – and external affairs, which were to remain under the control of what was then the Imperial Parliament. Similar guidance comes from looking at the division of powers in such countries as the USA and Canada, where external affairs are the responsibility of the federal government. There are good reasons for this, as relations with other countries need to be conducted on behalf of the whole nation, and it is not feasible for different parts of a country to have their own foreign policy. This also applies to related areas of policy, such as international aid and trade.

The aim of foreign policy is to promote and protect the interests of the whole country, and being part of the UK has given Scotland a far wider reach than it could hope to have as an independent nation. The UK has one of the largest global networks of diplomatic missions, with consular representation at 216 posts in 144 states, providing protection to British citizens living or visiting overseas. Scottish businesses also benefit from the support provided by UK Trade and Investment (UKTI), which has over 160 offices spread across more than 100 countries. In fact, Scotland has the best of both worlds, with specific support for Scottish exports provided through a partnership between UKTI and Scottish Development International (SDI), which has 26 offices in 15 countries outside the UK.

The UK's interests and security are enhanced by its global influence, demonstrated by the fact that it is a permanent member of the UN Security Council, NATO, the G7, G8, G20 and the Commonwealth. The UK is also the second-largest aid donor in the world, enabling it to play a prominent role in relieving poverty, saving lives during humanitarian crises and participating in peacekeeping missions.

In the post-Brexit world, assuming the UK leaves the European Union Customs Union – which imposes blanket EU rules regarding tariffs, quotas and restrictions relating to country of origin – it will also regain full control over trade policy. As with other aspects of foreign policy, the signing of trade treaties is best done on behalf of the country as a whole. Thus, in a Home Rule settlement, international trade would be a UK responsibility, and there would be a UK customs union governing customs procedures. However, given the overlap with devolved policy in relation to the economy and trade treaties, it is vital that a suitable mechanism exists to ensure Scottish input into UK policy.

4. The Home Civil Service

UK civil service (UK)
Currently, the entire civil service – including the Home Civil Service and the Diplomatic Service – is a reserved matter. Under a Home Rule settlement, where the UK civil service is working in reserved areas, this should continue to be the responsibility of the UK government.

Scottish civil service (Scotland)
The current reservation of the Home Civil Service includes the staff and statutory office-holders of the Scottish Administration. This means that Scottish Parliament cannot legislate about matters relating to civil servants in Scotland, including their recruitment, selection, management, conduct, discipline, numbers, grading and terms and conditions of service. The only current exceptions to this relate to court staff, such as sheriff clerks, procurators fiscal, and officers and staff of the High Court of Justiciary and Court of Session. Although they are part of the Home Civil Service, certain aspects of their appointment are peculiarly Scottish and so legislative competence is not reserved.

Under a Home Rule settlement, full responsibility for civil servants, staff and statutory office-holders working for the Scottish Administration should be transferred to the Scottish government. In assuming responsibility for all aspects of the employment of such civil servants, arrangements would need to be put in place to protect any pension entitlements already accrued.

5. Defence of the Realm (UK)

Defence spending in the UK is just under £40 billion – an amount that is far higher than would be possible in an independent Scotland. Scotland plays an integral part in all aspects of the UK's defence and benefits from this high level of spending, which, by its nature, contributes to protecting citizens across the entire UK. The defence budget also contributes significantly to Scotland's economy and employment of its workers.

The UK's size means it does not have to rely on the goodwill of allies as smaller countries do, and can operate independently in defence of its interests if necessary. Even so, it has built up a global network of alliances and partnerships, providing further security for the whole of the UK – Scotland included. This also means the UK can help to prevent or resolve conflicts overseas, as well as contribute to humanitarian operations.

In common with areas related to international relations, previous Home Rule proposals have always envisaged defence as being the responsibility of the UK. Furthermore, defence is a function exercised at a federal level in other federalised countries. Thus, for all the reasons outlined above, defence should remain the responsibility of the UK government.

6. Treason (UK)

The Treason Act 1351 sets out what offences are to be defined as treason, such as levying war against the sovereign. Since the Crown is a reserved matter, and there is no separate Scottish law of treason, treason should continue to be a reserved matter

Specific Reservations

The specific reservations in Schedule 5 of the Scotland Act 1998 (as amended in 2012 and 2016) are set out under 11 'Heads'. These are labelled A to L and correspond to particular areas of social and economic policy reserved to Westminster. Following the principle that there should be a presumption in favour of devolving responsibilities, many of these areas would become the responsibility of the Scottish Parliament under a Home Rule settlement. There are, however, important exceptions to this, which are discussed below. As with the general reservations, a suggestion is given in parentheses – either for the specific reservation in its entirety, or for particular areas within it – as to whether the powers should lie with the UK or Scotland.

Head A
Financial and Economic Matters (fiscal – except devolved taxes – economic
and monetary policy; currency; financial services;, financial markets; money
laundering)

Fiscal policy (UK)

The UK government would have the power to levy any tax in Scotland to meet its own spending in, or on behalf of, Scotland. This is in line with the principle that levels of government should be accountable for their own spending. The UK government would need to be mindful that particular taxes did not disproportionately affect Scotland. For instance, if government revenue was largely raised by a UK-wide tax on oil and whisky, then this would inevitably have a disproportionate effect on Scotland. However, this could be monitored by the Joint Ministerial Committee under its remit of coordinating the overall relationship between the UK and Scotland following Home Rule. Overall, the fiscal responsibilities of the UK government would be much reduced under Home Rule, though it would still be responsible for important areas of spending – such as defence – and would have to justify the form and level of any taxes levied to meet expenditure in, and on behalf of, Scotland.

Under Home Rule, should the UK government levy a particular tax, this would not prevent the Scottish government from levying the same type of tax, nor introducing any other tax it wished to. So, for example, both levels of government could levy an income tax on people in Scotland in order to meet their respective expenditure needs. The UK government would also be responsible for collecting any UK taxes levied in Scotland, thereby ensuring it is accountable for any inefficiencies in the system or collection services. However, it could choose, if it wished, to subcontract the collection of these taxes to the Scottish government.

Additionally, as part of its macro-economic management role, the UK government would need to take into account the different economies of the UK's constituent parts. To ensure fairness in this respect, the UK government would be responsible for administering a social cohesion fund to equalise resources across the UK. This would be based on need and would require clear and transparent rules.

Fiscal policy (Scotland)

Control over limited elements of fiscal policy has already been devolved to the Scottish level. This includes the ability to set income tax rates and thresholds; complete control over air passenger duty, aggregates levy, stamp duty land tax and landfill tax; partial assignment of VAT; and borrowing powers of up to £2.2 billion for capital spending and £500 million for revenue spending. These powers should be expanded to give the Scottish Parliament much wider discretion in fiscal policy. Essentially, Scotland should be responsible for setting the types, bands and rates of tax necessary to meet domestic expenditure. This is a very different principle from that applied to the current fiscal powers devolved to Scotland, whereby tax is tightly prescribed and the Scottish government is denied, for example, the ability to change income tax banding.

As mentioned above, under Home Rule the Scottish government could choose to levy the same types of tax as imposed by the UK government. This would allow the Scottish government to determine the structure of the taxation system in Scotland, as well as the level of borrowing required to meet expenditure needs. It would also have control over the allocation of resources, though its public spending would have to adhere to rules on overall public expenditure set at the UK level. Such rules are essential to the successful operation of a monetary union, and would be similar to the growth and stability pact rules set out for EU countries using the euro.

Economic policy (UK)

It is vital to the continued prosperity of those living in Scotland that there is free movement of people, goods, services and capital throughout the UK. In any Home Rule settlement, the UK will continue to be a single country and customs union, thereby preventing any potential barriers being erected. The main issue arising relates to the legal and regulatory framework, particularly in areas such as financial services. Scotland has always had its own legal system and, since regaining its own legislature in 1999, has implemented Scottish laws and regulations in devolved areas. Under Home Rule, this would be extended to cover all areas of policy decided at the Scottish level.

This legal and regulatory autonomy would be underpinned by a UK-wide principle of mutual recognition, in which both the UK and Scotland settled on agreed regulatory objectives. However, the means by which these objectives would be met need not be identical. Such mutual recognition would only cease to apply if one party could demonstrate that the other was in breach of the agreed objectives, in terms of, for example, public health, consumer or environmental protection. This is the principle currently underpinning the trade in goods across the EU, whereby if particular goods can be legally sold in one country within the union, they are deemed to be legal in other EU countries as well. In the UK, this principle should apply across all goods and services (including financial services), and would cover regulations governing standards, including the licensing and certification of products and professions. This principle would be legally enforceable through the Supreme Court, which would act as the arbiter in any constitutional disputes.

Monetary policy and currency (UK)

The UK has effectively been a monetary union since the Bank Charter Act of 1844 (1845 in Scotland), after which all new notes had to be backed on a one-for-one basis by Bank of England notes, which were the only legal tender. Thus, the Bank of England acquired a monopoly on issuing notes. Given that so much of Scotland's trade is with the rest of the UK, monetary union, including sharing a currency, makes economic sense. However, monetary union means there can only be one monetary policy, which must be at the UK level. This means the Bank of England, as the UK's central bank, would set the rules governing debt limits and interest rates. This would not preclude there being a Scottish central bank, which could be responsible for financing any deficit that arises over expenditure in Scotland, though this would have to be done within the overall framework of UK rules governing public expenditure.

Financial services, financial markets and money laundering (Scotland)

Harmonisation of regulations across the UK is not necessary for a single UK market to operate. Instead, this would be underpinned by the principle of mutual recognition. It would therefore be up to the Scottish government to decide whether it wished to keep its regulations – for example, those related to banking – identical to those of the rest of the UK, or to diverge.

Head B
Home Affairs (misuse of drugs; data protection and access to information; elections to the House of Commons; firearms – except air weapons – entertainment; immigration and nationality; scientific procedures on live animals; national security, official secrets and terrorism; betting, gaming and lotteries; emergency powers; extradition; lieutenancies; access to non-Scottish public bodies)

Misuse of drugs (Scotland)
Since crime and the justice system are the responsibility of the Scottish government, it seems anomalous that criminal law in relation to the misuse of drugs is currently reserved. In a Home Rule settlement, this anomaly would be removed.

Data protection and access to information (Scotland)
This area is currently governed by UK and EU legislation. There is no reason why Scotland should not set its own laws in this area, even if a decision is made to replicate UK law.

Elections to the House of Commons (UK)
The conduct of UK-wide elections must be decided at the UK level, as such elections affect the whole country. Furthermore, the rules of such elections need to be consistent, with the process agreed and accepted by all parts of the UK.

Firearms (Scotland)
As with other areas of criminal law, there is no need for this area of law to be determined on a UK-wide basis. Responsibility in relation to air weapons has already been transferred to the Scottish Parliament, and the rest of the law in relation to firearms should follow.

Entertainment (Scotland)
This reservation covers the licensing of premises for film exhibition and the classification of films. This classification is currently carried out by the British Board of Film Classification (BBFC), a non-statutory body set up by the film industry in 1912. These functions do not need to be carried out on a UK-wide basis and so would be transferred to the Scottish Parliament, which may well choose, for reasons of expediency, that it wishes the BBFC to continue in this role. However, this would be up to the Scottish Parliament to decide.

Immigration and nationality (UK)

It has become increasingly important for nation states to control their borders due to the large numbers of people moving from country to country and heightened security risks associated with international terrorism. Such issues were not so prominent when Home Rule was first proposed in the late 19th and early 20th centuries, as relatively few people travelled or moved to other countries, and international terrorism was virtually non-existent.

This has all changed and policy in relation to immigration and nationality is best decided at a UK-wide level, to ensure a broadly similar approach is adopted. This would mean citizenship rules would be determined for the whole of the UK, and there would also be a broad UK policy regarding immigration. However, given the importance of this area of policy for Scotland, there must be a mechanism for ensuring Scottish input into UK policy through the Joint Ministerial Committee. There is also scope for flexibility within this UK policy framework, as demonstrated in countries such as Australia and Canada. There are a number of possible options that would enable Scotland to differentiate its immigration policies in order to meet local demographic and labour needs, and these should be explored.

One such option relates to work permits, which would remain a UK responsibility, but with authority designated to Scotland, in recognition of the fact that this is an area falling on the borderline of UK and Scottish authority. On the one hand, it can be argued that work permits should come under immigration policy and border control, while on the other, responsibility for Scottish economic growth and its labour force is devolved. One of the most important factors for Scottish growth – as it is in any part of the world – is access to the required workforce, particularly workers with the necessary skills to deliver private, third sector and public sector services. There are a number of sectors in Scotland that have different requirements for work permits, such as:

- **Farming**, especially fruit farming in Perthshire, which requires a significant seasonal workforce to pick fruit.
- **The tourist sector**, which requires skilled hotel/restaurant managers and staff to operate destinations across the country, particularly where linguistic skills are required.
- **Care and nursing homes**, where there has been a shortage of local skilled workers.
- **The research and development sector**, where access to the

best minds from around the world is key to success in both
universities and corporate research departments.

Additionally, Scotland can attract some of the best students from around
the world to its universities, who in turn make a significant contribution to
the Scottish economy while learning the local language and culture. A Scottish government may wish to have the ability to offer these students a work
permit encouraging them to stay after they have finished their course.
Currently, there is a UK two-year work permit scheme for students.
However, employees usually only start to become truly valuable after training, which can often take at least two years, meaning those on this permit
scheme will have to leave the UK workforce just as they are really starting
to contribute to the economy.

Between 2005 and 2008, more than 8,000 students in Scotland benefited
from the Fresh Talent scheme, started by Jack McConnell when he was
First Minister. This was also limited to two years. Thus, when he became
First Minister, Alex Salmond approached the Home Office to request that
this time limit be removed. The Home Office, though, was concerned that
individuals might use the work permit in other parts of the UK. However,
an important change that came into effect in 2019 was that all Scottish
workers must be identified as such, in order that Scottish income tax can
be applied to them. This means there is now a system whereby Scottish
work permits could be awarded without them being valid outside Scotland.

One way of addressing the tension between Scottish requirements for
labour and UK controls over immigration is to implement a system similar
to that operating in Australia, which involves 'Designated Area Migration
Agreements' (DAMAs). This is a formal agreement – typically lasting five
years – between the Australian government and a designated area representative, usually a state or territory government, which sets out such
matters as occupations to be covered. There is then a second tier of individual agreements between the Australian government and individual
employers in the region, governed by the overarching agreement. This
means that DAMAs are not separate visas, but use the existing national
'Temporary Skills Shortage' and 'Employer Nominated Scheme' visa
programmes. The scheme enables employers in designated areas that are
experiencing skills and labour shortages to sponsor overseas workers.
However, in order to be eligible for the DAMA, an employer must be
endorsed by the state or territory government, and must demonstrate it has
made a genuine attempt to recruit Australians. This system provides flex-

ibility and is responsive to the needs of regional labour markets.

Under such a scheme, the UK and Scottish governments could enter into an overarching agreement allowing designated employers in Scotland to apply for work permits for overseas workers, in occupations where there is a shortage of workers. The agreement could be reviewed on a regular basis by the Joint Ministerial Committee, or any alternative structure that replaces it, to ensure it is appropriate and working effectively within the overall parameters of UK immigration policy.

Scientific procedures on live animals (Scotland)

This does not need to be determined at a UK level, though it would be expected that Scotland would wish to enact a similar – if not identical – law covering this area. Again, the key point is that Scotland is free to choose a different path should it wish to.

National security, official secrets and terrorism (UK)

Terrorism, as well as cyber, serious and organised crime, are best dealt with on a UK-wide basis, meaning that Scotland benefits greatly from the work of the UK's security and intelligence agencies. This is due both to the larger budget at the disposal of the UK's intelligence and security agencies, and also the global network of partnerships and alliances enjoyed by the UK, including the 'five eyes' intelligence-sharing arrangement.

Betting, gaming and lotteries (Scotland)

As with other areas of regulation, this does not require a UK-wide approach and so should be decided at the Scottish level. However, responsibility for the National Lottery would remain a reserved function, with it then being up to the Scottish government to decide if Scotland wished to remain a part of it or set up a Scottish lottery. National Lottery funding is currently distributed through both UK-wide and Scottish bodies. Again, it would be up to the Scottish government whether it wanted to agree a UK-wide arrangement for co-operation or make alternative arrangements.

Emergency powers (UK)

Emergency powers are designed to deal with a national crisis or emergency, and includes measures needed to preserve peace, as well as secure and distribute food, water, etc. It can involve deploying the armed forces and is therefore linked to reserved defence powers. These powers should, therefore, remain reserved.

Extradition (UK)

This is the process by which a person is surrendered by one state to another, in order to face trial in that country. As such, it is linked to international relations and so should remain a reserved matter.

Lieutenancies (Scotland)

These largely ceremonial roles involve representing the Crown on various occasions. The reservation applies to the division of Scotland into areas for lieutenancy purposes, their appointment and removal, and their functions and privileges. All these functions can be done in Scotland and do not need to be reserved.

Access to non-Scottish public bodies (UK)

This reservation limits the extent to which the Scottish Parliament can legislate about public access to information held by public bodies. Essentially, it means the Scottish Parliament can legislate on freedom of information for Scottish public bodies, including reserved information held by those bodies, while the UK government legislates for non-Scottish public bodies. However, any information provided by UK ministers or a UK government department in confidence is also reserved. This balance would need to be preserved in any Home Rule settlement.

Head C

Trade and Industry (business associations; insolvency; competition; intellectual property; import and export control; sea fishing outside the Scottish zone; consumer protection; product standards, safety and liability; weights and measures; telecommunications; postal services; research councils; designation of assisted areas; industrial development; protection of trading and economic interests) (Scotland)

The justification for the above trade and industry functions – most of which concern the regulation of a range of economic activities – being reserved is that there is a need for harmonisation across the UK. However, as discussed earlier, the mandatory harmonisation of regulatory functions is not a prerequisite for a single market to operate efficiently in the UK. Instead, all that is needed is agreement on the objectives sought rather than the means used to achieve them. This principle of mutual recognition would allow for regulatory divergence should this be the democratic decision of the Scottish Parliament. However, if one side felt the other was moving away from the agreed objectives in order to gain a competitive advantage, the matter could be taken to the Supreme Court.

Under a Home Rule settlement, Scotland and the rest of the UK would be starting from a position where their regulations were identical in all these areas. The Scottish Parliament could maintain regulatory alignment with the rest of the UK if it wished, but would be free to diverge if it thought it could achieve the same ends in a more effective manner. In this way, Scotland and the rest of the UK could learn from each other, potentially leading to better regulation all round.

There are other areas, such as the research councils, where continued co-operation between Scotland and the rest of the UK may well be beneficial. The Scottish Parliament is already able to legislate on the funding of research (including scientific), and to establish bodies that carry out, administer or fund such research. Under Home Rule, this responsibility would be extended to cover those research councils that are currently reserved. Even so, there would be plenty of scope for co-operation on projects between Scottish research bodies and their counterparts in the rest of the UK. In such cases, collaboration would involve a genuine partnership and be entered into on a voluntary basis, in areas of mutual benefit.

Scotland has a different economy to other parts of the UK, including sectors and industries that are uniquely important to it. Thus, it is logical that supporting and stimulating growth in the domestic economy should, under Home Rule, be the responsibility of the Scottish Parliament.

Head D
Energy (electricity; oil and gas; coal, nuclear energy; energy conservation)
(Scotland)

Under a Home Rule settlement, reserved functions in relation to energy would be transferred to the Scottish Parliament. Together with existing powers related to renewable energy and the environment, this would allow for the development of a coherent and sustainable approach to energy generation in Scotland.

The vast bulk of the North Sea oil and gas industry lies in the Scottish sector. This would become the responsibility of the Scottish government, which could then set the regulatory and fiscal regime, and collect the resultant revenues.

The Scottish government would also be able to decide whether to participate in the UK-wide market for electricity and gas. There are good reasons for doing so based on the integrated transmission networks between Scotland and the rest of the UK, and the mutual interest in sharing energy resources. However, it would be up to the Scottish and UK governments to develop a working partnership in relation to the energy market.

Head E
Transport (road transport; marine transport; air transport) (Scotland)

Under Home Rule, responsibility for transport in Scotland would pass to the Scottish Parliament. This would enable policy to be developed in line with Scottish needs and allow for coordination with linked areas of policy, such as the environment.

Given that most elements of transport policy are already controlled by the Scottish Parliament, extending this to transport links that are exclusively in Scotland should be reasonably straightforward. However, there would be a continuing need for policy coordination in relation to cross-border transport links and agencies. For example, while the awarding of franchises for the East Coast and West Coast mainlines would continue to be a matter for the UK government, under Home Rule there would be a greater role for the Scottish government in making such decisions. This would be laid out in any constitutional settlement.

Furthermore, the role played by UK-wide transport agencies in Scotland would be up to the Scottish government to decide. These bodies include motoring services agencies such as the Driver and Vehicle Licensing Agency (DVLA); maritime agencies such as the Maritime and Coastguard Agency; regulators such as the Office of Rail Regulation; and the provider of air traffic controller services, UK NATS. The Scottish government could either make arrangements with these bodies to continue providing their services in Scotland or institute a different way of delivering them. In the case of NATS, which is a public–private partnership, a Home Rule settlement could give the Scottish government a share of the UK government's stake. Such arrangements would ensure continuity, while giving the Scottish government the power to do things differently if it was felt this would improve Scotland's transport system.

Head F
Social Security (non-devolved social security schemes; child support; pensions)
(Scotland)

The Scotland Act 2016 gave the Scottish government responsibility for some social security benefits. As Professor Adam Tomkins sets out in a report entitled 'Shared Rule', responsibility was split between Westminster and the Scottish Parliament, with the former retaining control over the state pension, and the latter assuming responsibility for those with additional needs (for example, Carer's Allowance and Disability Living Allowance). The exception was Child Benefit, which remained reserved to Westminster.

Additionally, responsibility for Universal Credit – recently introduced by the UK government both to simplify the benefits system and help people move from welfare into work – is shared between Westminster and Holyrood. Universal Credit, which combines a number of benefits that were previously separate (for example, Housing Benefit, Jobseeker's Allowance and Child Tax Credit) falls under the overall responsibility of the UK Parliament. However, aspects of it – such as the frequency of payments and how it is paid – can be altered by the Scottish Parliament. The Scottish Parliament can also top up any benefit and create new benefits in devolved areas. As Professor Tomkins explains, this shared responsibility for welfare may cause distortions to the UK labour market if policy in Scotland diverges from that of the rest of the UK. This has knock-on consequences for Scottish and UK revenues. Tomkins argues that shared rule requires a new approach to devolution within the Union, including new mechanisms for dealing with inter-governmental relations.

There is certainly a strong case for improving inter-governmental relations, particularly in continuing areas of UK responsibility that overlap with Scottish responsibilities, which will be examined later. However, through a clear division of policy responsibilities, the Home Rule settlement proposed here seeks to remove, as far as possible, any issues arising from shared responsibility. In particular, this settlement proposes the transfer of two large areas of responsibility to the Scottish Parliament – that is, the ability to raise its own revenue and control over the reserved elements of social security.

While control over social security and pensions involves a massive transfer of spending power, it is in line with the subsidiarity principle as it is perfectly feasible to devolve this area of responsibility. This is demonstrated by the fact that social security (including pensions and child benefit) has been devolved in its entirety to Northern Ireland since 1998. It also makes sense, as many aspects of policy in relation to social protection and poverty alleviation – such as housing, health and social inclusion – are already devolved responsibilities. Similarly, working-age benefits and pensions are linked to other aspects of economic management that are largely devolved. In bringing these areas of policy together, Home Rule would allow for the adoption of coherent strategies that could effectively address such deep-seated issues. As such, the devolution of fiscal responsibility proposed in this book is essential. A long-term objective of social security reform has always been to integrate the tax and benefits system – Home Rule would help facilitate the achievement of this aim.

As with other areas of policy responsibility transferred to the Scottish Parliament under Home Rule, a different approach to welfare and pensions could be tried if so desired by the Scottish government, though existing contractual pension and benefit entitlements would have to be honoured. While a UK labour market would continue to operate, any consequences of a different welfare policy would be borne in Scotland, reinforced by the devolution of fiscal responsibility for Scottish spending.

Head G
Regulation of the Professions (architects; health professions; auditors) (Scotland)

As with other aspects of regulation, there is no requirement for uniformity in respect of these professions, provided the principle of mutual recognition applies. As this is currently a UK responsibility, the starting point would be identical regulation, with it then being up to the Scottish government to choose whether to diverge in any way.

Head H
Employment (employment and industrial relations; health and safety; non-devolved job search and support) (Scotland)

A Home Rule settlement would give transfer control of these employment issues to the Scottish Parliament, including areas such as industrial tribunals and the minimum wage. Given these areas do not need to be uniform across the UK, there is no compelling reason as to why decisions on them cannot be taken in Scotland. Either the UK approach can be replicated or a different Scottish approach put in place. Either way, the relevant decisions can and should be taken in Scotland, as this is an important area of policy with wider economic implications. Again, any divergence of approach would be protected by the principle of mutual recognition, whereby different laws or regulations in Scotland and the rest of the UK are respected as long as they seek to achieve the same goals. Any attempt by either side to move away from agreed objectives and to lower labour standards could be challenged in the Supreme Court.

Head J
Health and Medicines (xenotransplantation; embryology, surrogacy and genetics; medicines, medical supplies and poisons; welfare foods) (Scotland)

Given health is already a responsibility of the Scottish Parliament, these exceptions are unjustified and under Home Rule would no longer be reserved. There is no reason for a uniform UK approach to these areas of policy and, again, the principle of mutual recognition would apply to agreed common objectives regarding public health or consumer protection should the Scottish government choose to diverge from the rest of the UK.

Head K
Media and Culture (broadcasting; public lending right; government indemnity scheme; property accepted in satisfaction of tax) (Scotland)

Control over these areas of media and culture policy would cease to be reserved under a Home Rule settlement, with the main area of responsibility transferred being broadcasting. Regulation and licensing of all broadcasting would pass to the Scottish Parliament, with the handling of public service broadcasting a matter for the Scottish government to decide. While this could be done in conjunction with the BBC, the Scottish government would be free to explore other ways of fulfilling this responsibility.

Head L
Miscellaneous (judicial remuneration; equal opportunities; control of nuclear,
biological and chemical weapons and other weapons of mass destruction; Ordnance
Survey; time; outer space; Antarctica)

Judicial remuneration (Scotland)

This reservation applies only to the determination of certain senior judicial salaries in Scotland. Given the justice system is a Scottish responsibility, under Home Rule this function would no longer be reserved.

Equal opportunities (Scotland)

Equal opportunities is still largely a reserved area despite further powers being devolved under the Scotland Act 2016. This reservation largely covers the Equality and Human Rights Commission, created by the Equality Act 2006 and the Equality Act 2010, which consolidated a lot of previous anti-discrimination legislation. Under Home Rule, equal opportunities would cease to be reserved, with responsibility for this policy area resting with the Scottish Parliament.

Control of nuclear, biological and chemical weapons and other weapons of mass destruction (UK)

As this relates to matters of foreign relations and defence – in particular, the signing of international treaties – this would remain a reserved matter under Home Rule.

Ordnance Survey (Scotland)

Ordnance Survey is the national mapping organisation for Great Britain and the Isle of Man. Again, there is no reason responsibility for this needs to be reserved, and so under a Home Rule settlement it would become a Scottish responsibility (although coordination with the rest of Britain and the Isle of Man would be required).

Time (UK)

This reservation covers timescales, time zones, the determination of British Summer Time, the calendar, units of time and the date of Easter. Such issues are best decided at the UK level in order to ensure uniformity across the whole country, particularly regarding time zones.

Outer space (UK)

Under international law the UK is liable for damage caused through any activities in space, and so should remain responsible for the granting of licences to any UK body or person intending to carry out activities in outer space.

Antarctica (UK)

The Scotland Act 2012 added Antarctica to the list of reserved matters. In a Home Rule settlement, the UK government would continue to be responsible for the regulation of activities in Antarctica, as it is a political territory over which multiple countries share control. Thus, it falls under the UK's responsibility for international relations.

8
Financing Home Rule

The CSHR recognised that Home Rule must be underpinned by an appropriate fiscal settlement. Thus, its second core principle of fiscal responsibility stated that both the UK and Scottish governments should have the power to raise the revenue needed to meet their respective expenditures in, or on

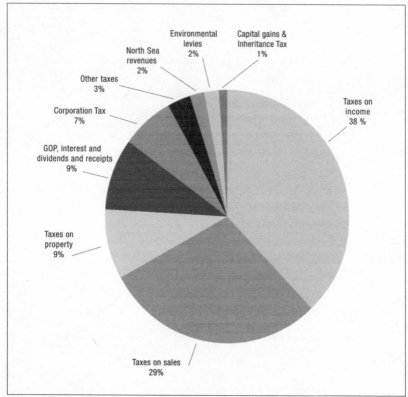

Figure 2. Scottish revenues 2018/19 according to form of taxation
Source: GERS, 2018/19

behalf of, Scotland. This is an important philosophical change from the current devolved arrangement, in which the UK Parliament has permitted specific taxes – the biggest being income tax – to be set in Scotland.

In analysing the current fiscal situation, it is helpful to highlight the problems inherent to the existing constitutional settlement. Figures 2 and 3 use the most recent Government Expenditure and Revenue in Scotland (GERS) statistics, with Figure 2 showing the proportion of revenue raised in Scotland by each of the various forms of taxation, and Figure 3 the proportions spent on each of the main areas of expenditure.

Figures 4 and 5 take this a stage further. Figure 4 on page 104 examines the proportion of revenue raised in Scotland in relation to how much is raised at the UK level from Scotland under various constitutional arrangements. Figure 5 on page 105, meanwhile, looks at the proportion of spend-

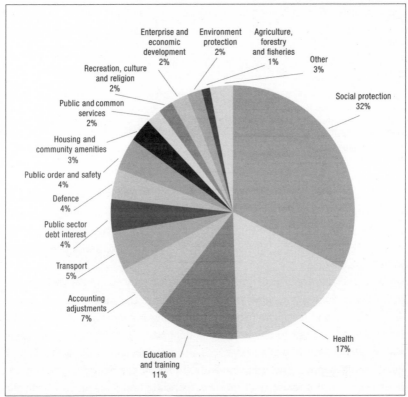

Figure 3. Scottish expenditure 2018/19 according to area

Source: GERS, 2018/19

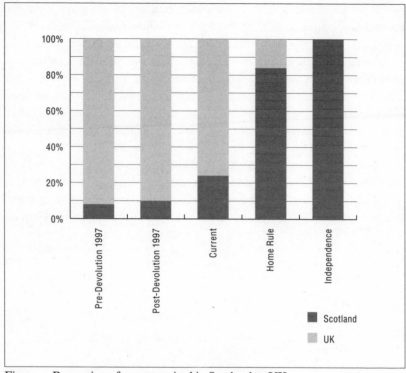

Figure 4. Proportion of revenue raised in Scotland vs UK
Source: GERS, 2018/19

ing in, and on behalf of, Scotland done at the Scottish level compared to the UK level. This shows that, following devolution, while the amount spent by the Scottish government is much higher, it is still not funding the majority of its spending. Instead, control of taxation remains overwhelmingly with Westminster.

When devolution was first implemented, the only tax power the Scottish government had was to alter the rate of income tax by 3 per cent. In the subsequent 20 years, more revenue-generating powers have shifted to the Scottish government to cover Scottish expenditure, particularly following the Scotland Acts of 2012 and 2016. Even so, this still falls well short of what would happen under Home Rule. In short, the Scottish government does not fund the majority of its own spending and so is not meeting the principle of fiscal responsibility. The next chapters look at how under Home Rule Scotland could move to a position of greater financial self-sufficiency.

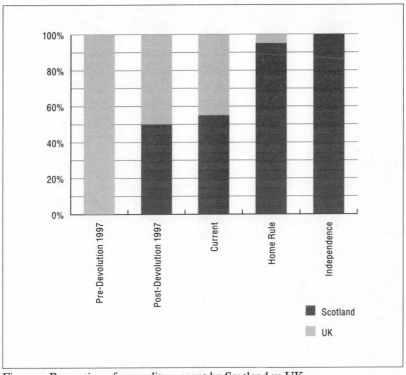

Figure 5. Proportion of expenditure spent by Scotland vs UK
Source: GERS, 2018/19

9
Fiscal Power

It is useful here to examine the concept of fiscal responsibility, or 'fiscal power', broadly defined as the responsibility for setting and collecting taxation. Each level of government has different levels of fiscal responsibility, with the strongest form of fiscal power being that of setting the level and bands of direct taxes without restrictions, as well as having the responsibility for collecting these taxes. For example, the UK government has unfettered authority to set the rates and bands of corporation tax in the UK, while the collection of the tax is the responsibility of HMRC, an agent of the UK government.

Of course, even a government with full fiscal powers is subject to controls, most notably at the ballot box. The public can be very sensitive to manifestos that propose increased tax levels or introducing new taxes that favour one section of society over another. It is widely accepted that a significant factor in Labour failing to win the 1992 general election was their leader Neil Kinnock announcing a proposed increase in the top rate of tax. Politicians recognise that headline rates of taxation – such as income tax – are sensitive, which is why they tend to rely on introducing new taxes, changing tax bands or indirect taxes. This can make for an overly complicated revenue collection system, and as a political approach often fails to work, as some new taxes can upset voters. For instance, Margaret Thatcher's popularity, particularly in Scotland, was significantly dented by the Poll Tax. Governments' fiscal powers in a democracy are, therefore, restricted by the need for public approval.

In addition, governments are restricted by competition from other countries, with individuals – as well as the businesses they own – able to move to lower tax environments should they wish. Following France's 2013 Finance Bill, which included significant tax increases, the estimated number of tax exiles leaving the county rose to 5,000, compared to just 1,000 the year before. This has led to efforts to harmonise some aspects of tax, thereby reducing the benefits associated with tax havens and stemming the flow of tax exiles.

Regulations at a supranational level can involve restrictions on tax, with, for instance, VAT levels in the UK currently restricted by EU tax regulation. Thus, for all the reasons outlined above, although full fiscal power gives a government the greatest level of autonomy, this is not without both internal and external controls.

The weakest form of fiscal power is where a level of government is given a grant. In the case of the EU, virtually all of its income comes from grants negotiated with member states each year. In the UK, most local government income is derived from grants.

Somewhere between taxes and grants is a grey area of taxation where responsibility is split. An example of this is assigned taxation, whereby a region has a fixed percentage of a particular tax set and collected in that area by another level of government. An example of this would be VAT in Scotland. In this case, the Scottish government receives 50 per cent of all VAT receipts in Scotland, but the setting of VAT and its collection remains the responsibility of the UK government.

Needless to say, as soon as one scratches the surface of taxation things become more complicated. No two systems are the same, with a plethora of means available to divide fiscal powers between different levels of government. While some countries have very centralised fiscal policies, with most of their revenue set and collected by the national government before being distributed to sub-national levels of government through grants, others have more devolved policies, with sub-national governments responsible for raising large proportions of the revenue they need to meet local expenditure.

Figure 6 on page 108, compiled from 2005 OECD data, shows levels of sub-national taxation across the G30 countries. As can be seen, less than 5 per cent of total tax in the UK is raised at a sub-national level. At the other end of the scale, it can be seen that the three countries with the highest levels of sub-national tax as a percentage of total tax are federal: Canada, Switzerland and the USA.

Figure 7 on page 109 shows a similar set of OECD results, looking at the overall level of income received at a sub-national level as a percentage of total national income, broken down according to type of revenue. It is interesting to note that in only three countries – Switzerland, the USA and Spain, all federal or quasi-federal countries – does the sub-national level have responsibility for the majority of public sector revenues. Within the chart, the part of each bar representing 'intergovernmental grants' (that is, the level of central government grants) reveals the sub-national tier's level

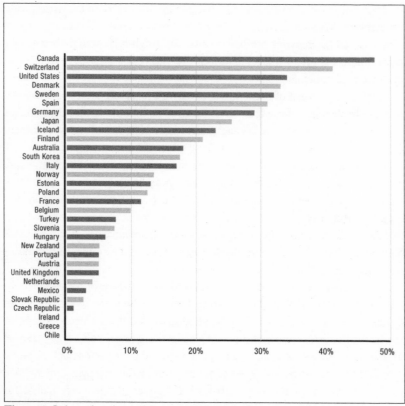

Figure 6. Sub-national taxation as a percentage of total taxation for G30 countries

Source: OECD figures, 2005

of dependence on the centre. Again, it can be seen that the UK has one of the highest proportions of sub-national revenue funded by central government grants.

What is evident from the above is that fiscal powers vary significantly across different countries. What is also clear is that the UK is one of the most centralised countries in the G30, with most fiscal power residing with the UK government. Less than 5 per cent of UK tax is raised at a sub-national level and across the UK local government is only responsible for spending about 30 per cent of total government income, with most of its

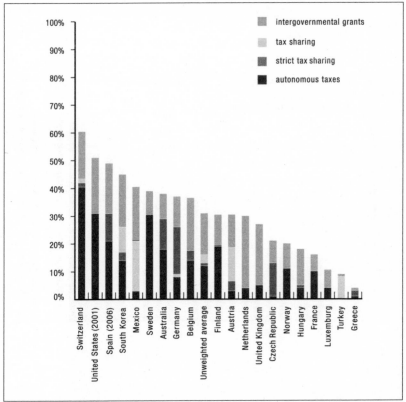

Figure 7. Sub-national government responsibility for revenue and source of revenue as a percentage of total public revenue

Source: Hansjörg Blöchliger and Oliver Petzold (2006), 'Finding the dividing line between tax sharing and grants', OECD

expenditure coming from paid income received as a grant from the centre.

A more recent chart (see Figure 8 on page 110), again from OECD data, confirms this by looking at the level of sub-national debt funded through central government grants. Again, as far as the UK is concerned, the data shows that the country is highly centralised in terms of fiscal powers. The old adage that 'He who pays the piper calls the tune' carries much truth. A structure of unitary government in which a high proportion of tax is raised centrally and then distributed as grants creates a sense of dependency on the centre, and a consequent lack of engagement at a local level.

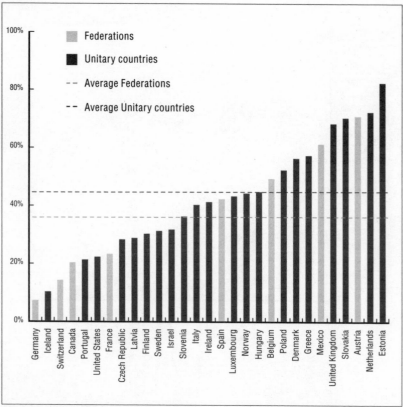

Figure 8. Vertical fiscal gaps across OECD countries (as percentage of sub-national governments' own spending, 2016 or latest data available)

Source: OECD Fiscal Decentralisation Database

10

The Pros and Cons of Devolving Fiscal Power

As Benjamin Franklin famously said, the only certainties in life are death and taxes. While few taxpayers like paying tax, there is, despite claims to the contrary in certain newspapers, a high degree of tax compliance in most developed countries. The question is whether taxation should be controlled and collected centrally or more locally.

Advocates of centralised tax systems put forward a number of arguments, the main one being that fiscal and monetary policy should be the responsibility of the same level of government. For most nations, monetary policy is set at a national level, for which there are good reasons. Control over currency at a national level makes sense, as it acts as a natural valve for economic change. If a country is performing badly then often its currency is devalued, enabling it to sell more goods abroad and attract foreign investment into the country. The controls around this, such as setting government borrowing rates and issuing more currency, help to provide balance and so stabilise an economy. When different areas are part of the same currency zone, there needs to be a level of social support and workforce mobility that allows the success of one area to mitigate problems in another. The USA is a good example of migration within a currency zone, with people migrating to states that are economically booming – this can be seen, for instance, in the huge movement of people from the Midwest to California in the 1950s and 60s. Further, central government will support struggling areas through fiscal transfers, as this is part of the social bond of belonging to a nation.

The eurozone is an exception to this link between the nation state and a currency. It is yet to be seen whether the euro will work in the long run without greater federalisation across the EU. Although there are no regulatory barriers to the movement of people, there are language and other cultural barriers restricting workforce movement from one EU state to another. In addition, there is a reluctance to cross-subsidise or 'bail out' an ailing state. The example of Greece over the past decade is a case in point. The problems faced by Greece have not been helped by a strong euro, as if it still had its own currency, this might have been devalued to allow a rebalancing of the economy. These issues will be examined in greater detail below, when the Social Cohesion Fund is discussed.

Given monetary policy is usually under national control, the argument goes that national governments should also have control of fiscal policy, in order that both can be used to manage and stimulate the economy. On top of this, there are other arguments for a centralised fiscal policy, one of which is that having lots of different taxes at different levels of government creates an overly complicated system. However, the UK itself demonstrates, centralisation is no guarantee of simplicity. In 2009, it was reported that the UK tax code had exceeded that of India, its 11,520 pages making it the longest in the world.

Another argument put forward in favour of centralising fiscal powers is tax harmonisation, thereby avoiding tax competition that leads to a 'race to the bottom'. The contention is that tax competition drives taxes down to the point where there is insufficient public revenue to support public services. An oft-quoted example is that of corporation tax, where different countries and regions slash tax rates in order to entice companies to move their headquarters there.

Generally speaking, though, the public accepts the need for taxation, with the pressure for good public services balancing any desire to reduce the tax take as a percentage of gross domestic product (GDP). For this reason, countries do not race to the bottom. Instead, tax revenue is largely contained in a band between 25 per cent and 45 per cent of GDP, as shown in Figure 9 on page 113.

A final argument deployed in favour of greater tax centralisation is that fiscal powers can be used to create social unity and equality across a nation. This argument extends beyond fiscal powers to centralisation generally, including health, education and policing, the claim being that the public benefits from similar standards across all services. However, centralised uniformity does not, in itself, lead to improvements in public services or greater fairness. This is because differences exist across the various parts of a country. Treating them in the same way will not deliver policies that are right for all areas, whereas enabling each area to adopt its own approach to taxation or public service delivery tends to lead to higher standards and fairer outcomes. This is why greater centralisation across the board in order to facilitate equality is not a policy currently supported by any of the main UK political parties. Instead, all favour local government and support – at

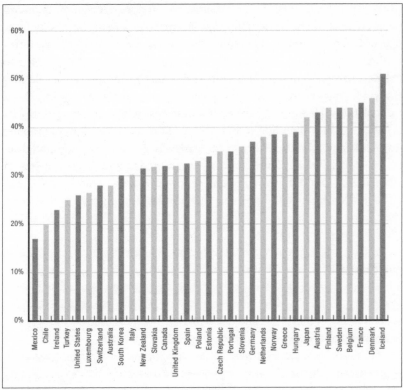

Figure 9. Tax revenue as a percentage of GDP for G30 countries
Source: OECD figures

a minimum – current levels of devolution. It is also important to remember that the British Isles already contain a number of Crown dependencies, such as Jersey, Guernsey and the Isle of Man, which have existed quite comfortably alongside the rest of the UK despite having completely different tax regimes.

What, then, are the arguments for greater devolution of fiscal powers to sub-national tiers of government? Perhaps the most powerful relates to responsibility and accountability. When a particular level of government only controls spending on public sector services, with limited or non-existent revenue-raising responsibility, this both greatly reduces accountability and changes attitudes towards spending. In this regard, an analogy that might be used is of the difference in attitude a teenager might display if they were to be given either £10 worth of sweets, £10 worth of pocket money to buy sweets, or have to earn the £10 themselves. Before devolution, Scotland received most public services through Westminster and the Scottish Office, part of UK government. Therefore, there was a dependency on Westminster. After devolution, the majority of domestic spending was devolved to the Scottish government, but with very limited revenue-raising powers alongside this, thereby creating spending responsibility without fiscal responsibility. However, Home Rule would ensure that fiscal responsibility broadly matches spending responsibility. This creates real accountability for politicians, who then have to set tax levels to match spending requirements. Thus, if the Scottish government wanted to spend more or less on education, it could do by increasing or lowering the tax rates, rather than raiding other budgets. Voters can then decide at the ballot box whether they agree with the spending choices of politicians relative to the public money required to fund them.

In fact, this approach should apply at all levels of government. Local government in Scotland has responsibility for council tax, which represents less than 20 per cent of local government expenditure. Nor is it not only about sub-national government either – part of the reason the EU lacks accountability is that it sets and raises no direct tax, instead relying on grants from member countries to cover its expenditure budget.

Another argument in favour of tax devolution is it creates a tax environment suitable for the economy of the area. Different parts of a country may wish to encourage different industries and stimulate the economy in different ways. Fiscal stimulus is a useful way to do this. In this regard, it is instructive to look at the example of the USA, with Figure 10 on page 115 showing the split of different types of taxes between states.

The range of taxes varies from state to state in order to suit local preference and a particular state's economy. Even states that lie next door to each other can have radically different tax breakdowns. Take Nevada and Oregon, both of which have comparable populations to Scotland, a GDP per head of $50,000, and around 5 per cent unemployment. However, when it comes to type of taxes, Oregon raises almost 50 per cent of its state tax revenues through income tax and corporation tax, while Nevada raises none through these methods, instead relying on high property and sales taxes. Of course, the main industries in the two states are very different. Oregon's largest industry is advanced manufacturing and taxes are designed to encourage this sector, whereas in Nevada the main industry is tourism.

Both in terms of employment and economic size, Scotland's main industry sector is financial and business services. This is followed by tourism in

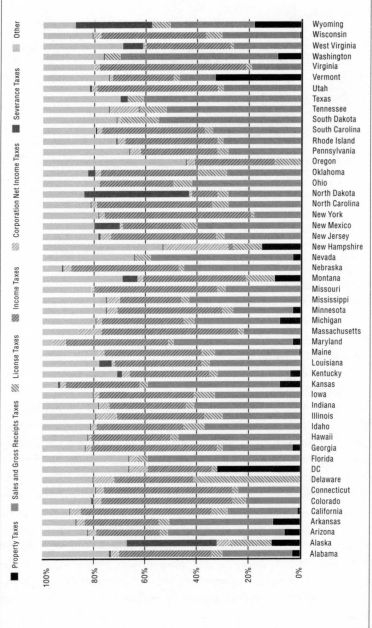

Figure 10. Collections by tax type as a percentage of total state tax revenue collections

Source: US Census Bureau, BofA Merrill Lynch Global Research

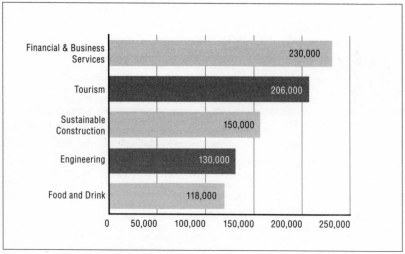

Figure 11. Top 5 employment sectors in Scotland
Source: Scottish Enterprise, April 2019

terms of employment, and energy in terms of economic size, as shown in Figure 11. Therefore, a key argument for devolving powers is that this would allow a tax system to be designed that would be fully suitable for the Scottish economy.

In addition to creating taxes suitable for local economies, there is also a social element to tax, with different countries and regions having different attitudes regarding appropriate levels of tax and wealth redistribution. Much has been made of the Scandinavian model in this regard, particularly by the pro-independence parties in Scotland. It is true that Scandinavian countries have traditionally had a high tax-to-GDP ratio compared to other European counties, although this has fallen in the past decade, and France and Belgium currently have a higher ratio than Norway, Sweden and Finland. The Scandinavians' relatively larger public sector may be partly due to a higher level of social acceptance to wealth distribution, though for the majority of the past ten years Scandinavian countries have had more right-of-centre governments than left-of-centre. However, it may also be due to the high level of decentralised taxation, which means that people accept taxation more readily because they can see the money they pay being spent locally on things such as schools, community health centres and infrastructure.

Scotland has traditionally been a more left-of-centre country, certainly over the past 50 years in political terms. This perhaps reflects differing social attitudes towards equality. While this should not be overplayed – social surveys suggest people in Scotland share many similar views with the rest of the UK – it is certainly a factor in choosing a different tax environment for Scotland.

There is also an element of taxation that involves encouraging social change, particularly in relation to health and the environment. Different countries and regions face different issues in this regard. Scotland, for instance, has very high levels of diabetes, with over 15 per cent of NHS spending in Scotland currently going on Type 2 diabetes. A sugar tax may prove to be an additional weapon in the Scottish government's arsenal when tackling this problem, particularly as the health of its citizens is one of its key devolved responsibilities. On the environmental front, Scotland might recognise the need for cars in rural areas and, therefore, put in place a system of taxation sufficiently sophisticated to ensure that it tackles congestion in cities, while not penalising those in other parts of Scotland who have no option but to travel by car.

Lastly, there is the counter argument to the 'race to the bottom', which is that competition is healthy for the consumer. This view was set out succinctly by one of the greatest of all Scots, Adam Smith, who stated: 'In general, if any branch of trade, or any division of labour, be advantageous to the public, the freer and more general the competition, it will always be the more so.' Tax competition has the potential to drive accountability and efficiency, and is therefore good for UK citizens as consumers of public services.

In this regard, Switzerland provides a useful example. Within the Swiss federation, different cantons compete to attract different segments of the economy, whether commuters, tourists, manufacturers or financiers. It has created not only healthy competition but a healthy economy. Although of course there are many other factors involved, it should be noted that Switzerland is one of the three wealthiest nations on earth in terms of GDP per head.

II

A Fiscal Settlement for Home Rule

The Home Rule settlement proposed here recognises the importance of devolved tax powers, on the basis that different levels of government should, as far as possible, be responsible for raising the money they spend. This will in turn make them genuinely accountable to the electorate for the policies they implement in the areas they control.

The fiscal settlement for Home Rule would be part of a new written constitution governing the relationship between Scotland and the rest of the UK. As in other areas, this would set out what would remain reserved matters for the UK government, with everything else automatically devolved. This would give the UK government the power to levy any tax needed to meet its own spending in or on behalf of people in Scotland. This is in line with the Campaign for Scottish Home Rule (CSHR) principle that each level of government should be responsible and accountable for its own spending. Following on from this, the UK government would have to justify the form and level of any taxes it levied to meets its expenditure in, and on behalf of, Scotland. However, as mentioned earlier in the book, the constitution would make clear that the UK levying a particular tax would not in any way prevent the Scottish government from levying the same type of tax.

Home Rule would, therefore, address one of the problems with fiscal devolution to Scotland as it currently stands, which is that only limited elements of fiscal policy have been devolved, thereby constraining the Scottish government's room for manoeuvre. For example, while the Scottish Parliament can set income tax rates, it cannot set bands; while Scotland receives tax on earned income, the opposite is true for investment income; and while Scotland receives 50 per cent of VAT receipts, it cannot change the rate of VAT. The current system is, therefore, a blunt instrument, with the Scottish government largely limited to putting taxes up or down.

Home Rule would give the Scottish government much wider discretion over fiscal policy, including the ability to determine the structure of the taxation system in Scotland and the level of borrowing required to meet its expenditure needs. However, public spending would have to be kept within rules on overall public expenditure set at the UK level. Such rules are essential to the successful operation of a monetary union, and would be similar to the growth and stability pact rules set out for EU countries using the euro.

Responsibility for tax collection would lie with the level of government setting the tax, though this does not mean it would necessarily collect the tax itself. For instance, the Scottish government could use HMRC to collect VAT. Conversely, given the bulk of tax will be the responsibility of the Scottish government, the UK government may choose to subcontract the collection of taxes due at a UK level to the Scottish government. Even so, the payment mechanism for the tax should be decided by, and the responsibility of, the level of government receiving the tax.

As mentioned earlier, rules would need to be put in place to ensure a particular UK tax did not disproportionately affect Scotland. Therefore, a UK tax on whisky and oil would need to be balanced by taxes on other goods in order to ensure that no UK region paid a disproportionate amount of UK taxation.

The system outlined above is similar to that which currently operates in Canada, where both the federal government and provincial/territorial governments have the power to raise taxes, meaning a federal and provincial income tax can exist side by side. This system works well and is the best way of ensuring that both levels of government can raise what they spend.

12

Social Cohesion Fund

Any Home Rule settlement would need some form of social cohesion fund underpinning it, the aim of which would be to ensure fairness and equalise resources across the UK. The UK government would be responsible for this as part of its role in macro-economic management, and in doing so would need to take into account the differing economies of the UK's constituent parts. The fund would require clear and transparent rules and be based strictly on need.

Without sufficient social and economic cohesion, no single currency zone or fixed exchange system can truly be stable. History is littered with attempts, such as the gold standard or the European Exchange Rate Mechanism (ERM), to achieve a long-term standard currency arrangement. Most, though, are unsuccessful unless there is real political integration. The reason for this is that currency is the last valve that can be used to adjust the relative wealth of an area and make it more competitive. Unless the entire currency area is prepared to manage different economic conditions across the same monetary zone, any significant shifts will create a strain on the monetary system.

This point is illustrated by the economic recession that took place in the wake of the 2007 banking crisis, specifically its impact on Greece and Iceland – the former country part of the eurozone, the latter with its own currency (the króna). When the banking crisis hit Iceland, its three major banks – Lansbanki, Kaupthing and Glitnir – went bankrupt, its GDP per head fell by over 40 per cent in the space of two years, and its stock market crashed by 90 per cent. Furthermore, the króna fell by nearly 50 per cent against the dollar and, following the crash, Iceland's government imposed capital controls to protect the value of the currency. After currency markets had stabilised the króna, its value remained relatively steady at around 120 króna against the dollar, compared to around 60 króna before the crisis. It could therefore be argued that the wealth of Icelanders had halved compared to Americans.

However, the fall in Iceland's currency was also its last defence. Though imports became more expensive and consumption of foreign goods fell, a stronger domestic market was created. More importantly, Icelandic exports became cheaper and, therefore, more competitive. At the same time, the relative value of Icelandic assets was now cheaper to foreign investors, resulting in capital flowing into the country without the need for price deflation. Now, ten or so years on from the crisis, Iceland's economy is growing strongly, with GDP per head as measured in dollars now 6.4 per cent higher than it was in 2007, before the crash.

Greece's story is rather different. Like Iceland, it was badly affected by the economic crisis, though its impact was only truly felt in 2009. Unemployment rose from 8 per cent to over 27 per cent, while GDP per head fell by 40 per cent over the next seven years. However, unlike the króna, the euro did not fall against the dollar, held up by the relative strength of eurozone countries such as Germany. Therefore, Greece was unable to benefit from any significant currency devaluation that would act as a pressure valve to help its failing economy.

In a country such as the USA, different areas do have very different economic cycles within a single currency zone. However, the USA enjoys far more social cohesion and people will move to an area that is performing well, which supports growth and reduces overall unemployment. Importantly, it is the federal government's duty is to ensure that relatively poor states or areas are supported through fiscal transfers and national economic programmes. Though the EU makes efforts towards these ends, cultural and language barriers make movement between countries harder, and there is far less central support for countries such as Greece. Resentment then builds up against countries within the eurozone, such as Germany, that benefit from the relative weakness of the euro compared to its economic growth. The words of Greece's former Finance Minister Yanis Varoufakis reflect this resentment:

Europe in its infinite wisdom decided to deal with this bankruptcy by loading the largest loan in human history on the weakest of shoulders ... What we've been having ever since is a kind of fiscal waterboarding that has turned this nation into a debt colony. [The eurozone] resembles a fine riverboat that was launched on a still ocean in 2000. And then the first storm that hit it, in 2008, started creating serious structural problems for it. We started leaking water. And of course, the people in the third class, as in the Titanic, start feeling the drowning effects first.

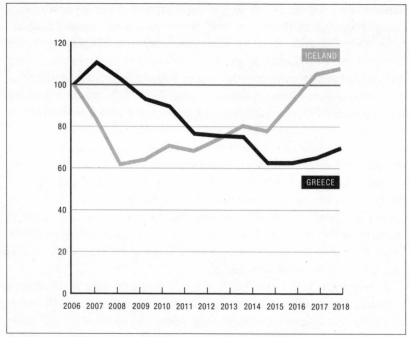

Figure 12. GDP per capita of Greece and Iceland, 2006–2018
Source: World Bank data

As illustrated by Figure 12 above, Greece – unlike Iceland – has not bounced back. Instead, its GDP remains 40 per cent lower than in 2007.

Although the various nations of the United Kingdom are justifiably proud of their respective traditions and differences, they also have much in common, including a shared language. There are few social barriers preventing a Scot from working in London or a Yorkshireman from living in Aberdeen, apart from some possible teasing about accents. Therefore, there is already healthy social cohesion within the sterling monetary zone. In addition, there is fiscal support, with no real resentment arising when the UK government supports areas that are struggling economically. For instance, over the last few decades Northern Ireland has seen a constant net inflow of funding from the rest of the UK. Under Home Rule, therefore, it is vital that both cultural and economic stability is maintained within a single monetary zone.

The shared cultural identity of the UK is both a key component of Home Rule and a key difference from independence, which would see the

UK cultural identity consigned to history. A Great Britain team at the Olympics and a joint national anthem are just the tip of the iceberg in terms of the historical and social links binding everyone together. Under Home Rule, these cultural bonds remain, even as the separate cultures of each part of the country are respected.

Equally important is economic stability. At present, 92 per cent of all taxation throughout the UK is raised by Westminster taxes. While this does bring economic cohesion, it comes at the cost of a heavy concentration of power. Under Home Rule, each level of government will be responsible for funding what it spends, meaning this element of economic cohesion will be lost. This is why a UK-wide economic mechanism for creating social cohesion is required.

Looking at Table 2 below, it can be seen that the deficit per head across the UK is significantly lower in England than in the other home countries. If the average deficit per head across the UK – which is funded through UK borrowing – is deducted from the deficit per head in each of the home countries, then England can be seen to be relatively supporting the rest of the UK. This is principally driven by London and the South-east, which has an overall surplus. The difference between the UK's constituent countries shows that if each is paid its share of average deficit funding after taking account of borrowing, England creates a surplus and the other nations are in deficit. This should come as no surprise, although there have been times over the past 20 years when Scotland would have had the surplus and

Table 2. UK deficit, deficit per head and net position in 2018/19 for the UK's constituent countries

Source: Office for National Statistics

	Deficit £bn	Deficit per head £bn	Net position per head £bn	Net position
England	32.8	-598	+503	+26.1
Scotland	15.5	-2,882	-1,781	-9.4
N. Ireland	9.15	-5,132	-4,031	-7.2
Wales	14.0	-4,502	-3,401	-10.5
Total UK	71.8	-1,101	0	0

England the deficit. The net difference has never been more than £30bn, which is only 4 per cent of all public expenditure, giving an indication of the extent of the problem. It also fluctuates from year to year.

Thus, under Home Rule, the UK government would have responsibility for a social cohesion fund addressing some of this difference. Each year, a limited proportion – say 2 per cent – of all UK public sector expenditure would be placed in the fund. Assuming a level of, say, 2 per cent of expenditure, this sum should not be so significant as to create resentment. At current levels, this represents about £15bn per year – the same size as current UK gross contributions to the EU (in 2018, this amounted to £17.4bn before the rebate). The allocation of the fund would be the responsibility of Westminster, distributed on a 'needs basis', rather than a Barnett Formula-esque allocation per head. A needs-based formula for funding involves money being allocated according to the specific needs of an area, such as addressing poor literacy, a high crime rate or low life expectancy.

Since 2007, the Welsh Parliament has done considerable work on needs-based criteria for funding, both in the Silk Commission and the Holtham Commission. In particular, the Holtham Commission's July 2010 report set out a possible needs-based formula, incorporating six indicators related to demographics, deprivation and costs that indicate the need for public services and greater funding. These were: 1) number of children; 2) number of older people; 3) ethnicity; 4) income poverty; 5) prevalence of ill health; and 6) sparsity of population.

Therefore, under Home Rule, a social cohesion fund using these or similar criteria could be used to fund areas in need of support. As things currently stand, the fund would essentially result in London subsidising less affluent parts of the UK. This redistribution of wealth would both bind the UK together, and ensure stability for a single monetary zone across the four nations.

13
Funding the Deficit

Any financial settlement for Home Rule will require agreement on address-ing Scotland's public spending deficit. At £2,882 per head in 2018/19, this is significantly higher than the UK average of £1,101 per head – something that may remain the case for the foreseeable future. When looking at deficits, it has been assumed throughout this book that Scotland would get its share of oil revenue based on geography rather than population, in the same way that any other mineral asset – such as coal – would be allocated across the UK to the area of production.

In recent years, the difference between Scotland's public spending deficit and the UK average as a percentage of GDP has been significant. However, this has not always been the case, as can be seen in Figure 13 on page 126.

There are essentially five ways to fund the deficit under Home Rule, outlined below:

1. Scotland's share of the UK deficit
The total UK deficit is the amount of expenditure the UK government cannot meet through its revenue. This is then funded by UK borrowing. UK borrowing is a reserved matter and the interest from UK borrowing is paid for from UK taxes, including under Home Rule, UK taxes raised in Scotland. Therefore, Scotland should get its percentage share per head of new UK debt to fund the UK deficit. The UK borrowed £1,101 per head across the UK to fund the deficit in 2018/19, therefore under Home Rule Scotland would have received its pro rata share of borrowing by population, which would be £6.1 billion. However, despite receiving its share of UK debt, this would still have left Scotland with a deficit per head of £1,781, or some £9.4bn in total, to fund.

2. Social cohesion fund
Under a 'needs-based' assessment, it is likely Scotland would receive a disproportionate amount of any social cohesion fund compared to England,

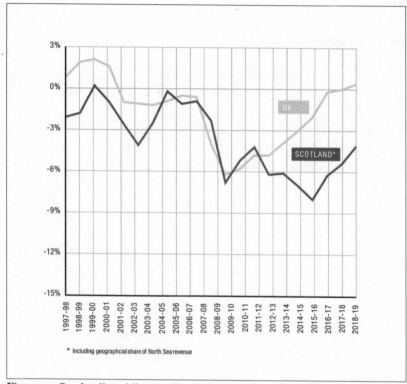

Figure 13. Scotland's public spending deficit compared to UK average as a percentage of GDP, 1997–2019

Source: GERS, 2018/19

particularly as it has a high percentage of rural and low-income areas. Given that the fund would need to be for the benefit of the whole of the UK, it is unlikely this would cover all of Scotland's remaining deficit (assuming 2018/19 levels and a social cohesion fund of £15bn).

3. Scottish borrowing
The Scottish government could itself borrow to fund the deficit, particularly for capital expenditure. There would, however, need to be limits on borrowing to avoid financial crisis and ensure sustainable public sector funding across the UK single monetary zone. The level of borrowing across the UK would therefore be monitored and delimited by Westminster and the Bank of England as part of its responsibility for monetary stability.

4. Increasing Scottish taxes

The Scottish Parliament could raise additional taxation to fund higher public sector expenditure. One of the advantages of Home Rule is that it allows Scotland to take fiscal responsibility, meaning that if the Scottish public voted for a government promising higher public expenditure, then this should lead to people in Scotland paying higher taxes. If tax levels are increased or new taxes introduced, then a Scottish government would need to be aware of any potentially counterproductive impacts this could have on Scotland's economy. The well-known Laffer curve effect – proposed by Art Laffer in 1974 – demonstrated that there comes a point at which further raising taxes produces less tax revenue.

5. Reduce expenditure

Every government would like to reduce public expenditure through being more efficient. Given that under Home Rule the Scottish government would have to fund its own spending, this should in theory make politicians more focused on avoiding wasteful expenditure. However, efficiency usually only reduces public expenditure at the margins. To avoid having to increase taxes to fund the remainder of the deficit, serious choices would need to be made about reducing public expenditure.

There is some comment in the English press about the unfairness of Scots getting prescriptions, eye tests and university tuition paid through the public sector, given taxes in England and Scotland are essentially the same. Home Rule would allow Scotland to decide what it provides for 'free' to the public at point of delivery, and would require the Scottish government to be accountable for funding it. This in turn would focus the minds of politicians on being prudent with taxpayers' money, thereby making them more fiscally responsible.

It should be remembered that if the Scottish economy performs well, then the tax revenues this would generate would allow greater public sector expenditure. A reinvigorated Scotland under Home Rule may even generate sufficient growth to create a surplus, or at least a better net fiscal balance per head than the rest of the UK. This would result in a virtuous circle, as Scotland would still receive its proportion of new UK debt.

14
A Scottish Treasury

Under Home Rule, the Scottish government would require significant additional resources to deal with the transfer of fiscal powers and meet its responsibilities in areas such as pensions and benefits. Presently, the Scottish government has a Finance Minister (or, to give the position its full title, the Cabinet Secretary for Finance, Economy and Fair Work), with responsibilities including the Scottish economy, inclusive growth, managing the public finances, fiscal policy and taxation, the Scottish budget, and budgetary monitoring and reporting. The Finance Minister is also responsible for Revenue Scotland, which was set up in 2012 to collect the limited number of devolved taxes. Full fiscal responsibility for Scottish expenditure would necessitate a proper Scottish Treasury, directly responsible to the Finance Minister. The Scottish Treasury would be required to carry out, amongst other things, the following five functions.

1. Setting tax
With a full range of taxes available to fund the Scottish budget under Home Rule, the Scottish Treasury would be required to produce a comprehensive package of taxation, including rates and bands. The Scottish Cabinet and, ultimately, the Scottish Parliament, would then be responsible for approving this. Within this process, the Scottish Treasury could propose new taxes, such as a sales tax or a wealth tax.

2. Tax and revenue collection
Setting fiscal policy should be linked with responsibility for revenue collection. The Scottish Treasury could delegate this to a third party, such as HMRC, or organise collection itself – this choice being the decision of the Scottish Parliament.

3. Scottish debt

The Scottish Treasury would be responsible for funding the Scottish deficit and capital expenditure. This would include providing guarantees and other support of debt. As already mentioned, the level of debt incurred by the Scottish Treasury would need to be monitored and delimited by Westminster and the Bank of England. The level of UK government support of the debt would also need to be determined, as this will affect the interest costs of borrowing.

4. Budget, accounting and audit

The Scottish Treasury would propose the annual budget, containing estimates of expenditure and revenue for the coming year, together with any changes in taxation. It would also be responsible for accounting and audit.

5. Liaison with the UK Treasury

Under Home Rule and a single currency zone, a degree of coordination between the Scottish and UK treasuries would be required in order to reduce inconsistencies and ensure the fairness of both tax systems. Additionally, fiscal policy impacts monetary policy, which would need to be monitored. Therefore, Westminster would provide input into the Scottish Treasury to ensure its policies were consistent with UK-wide monetary policy. Likewise, the Scottish Treasury would have representation in UK monetary policy discussions.

15

A Constitution for Home Rule

The third core principle set out by the Campaign for Scottish Home Rule (CSHR) was that the relationship between Scotland and the rest of the UK must be based on mutual respect. Contrary to this, the current settlement is based on an unequal relationship, as in a devolved system, sovereignty ultimately remains with Westminster. Under the Scotland Act 1998, Westminster retained the power to make laws for Scotland, although this was limited by application of the Sewel Convention. Named after Lord Sewel – the Scottish Office minister who announced the policy in the House of Lords during the passage of the 1998 Scotland Act – the convention states that Westminster will not normally legislate on devolved matters without the consent of the Scottish Parliament. This was put into statutory form in the 2016 Scotland Act.

The Scotland Act 2016 also sought to ensure the permanence of the Scottish Parliament by stipulating it could only be abolished should the people of Scotland vote for this outcome in a referendum. However, there is considerable doubt amongst academics and commentators over whether this is binding, as conventional constitutional theory suggests that a Westminster Parliament cannot tie its successors. This leaves open the possibility of the act's provisions being repealed or amended, though the political consequences of doing so make this highly unlikely.

Thus, to achieve the aims of securing the permanence of the Scottish Parliament, entrenching the respective powers of the UK and Scottish governments, and creating a relationship based on equality, a written constitution is required. This is something the Liberal Democrats, amongst others, have advocated for many years.

This written constitution, which would govern the relationship between Scotland and the rest of the UK, could in principle be a relatively simple document. When most people think of written constitutions, they think of the USA and the perceived difficulties this has caused – in particular, the enshrining of the 'right to bear arms', which has made it very difficult to introduce gun control reforms. This, though, is one of the first ten amendments to the US Constitution, known as the Bill of Rights, which offers specific protections regarding individual liberty while placing restrictions on the powers of the government. The basic constitution itself consists of seven articles setting out how government in the US should operate. Specifically, it clarifies the separation of powers between the different branches of federal government, as well as the respective powers of the federal government and individual states. It is something along these lines – setting out the respective powers of the UK and Scottish parliaments – that is required for Scottish Home Rule. This would be done on the basis laid out in Chapter 7, in terms of defining the powers reserved to the UK Parliament and everything else being left to the Scottish Parliament.

The key to ensuring any partnership of equals would be guaranteeing that the constitution could not be changed unilaterally by the UK Parliament. The constitution would need to be negotiated between Scotland and the rest of the UK on a bilateral basis, with any proposed amendments requiring the consent of both the UK and Scottish parliaments.

It should be noted that a constitution for Home Rule would only affect the relationship between Scotland and the rest of the UK – it would not require any change in relationship for other parts of the UK, such as Wales and Northern Ireland. In this, it differs from a fully-fledged federal system and so would be less disruptive, seeking instead to work through existing institutions.

In terms of how the UK Parliament would operate, Scottish MPs' participation would be restricted to those UK matters specified in the constitution. This addresses the current inequality that Scottish MPs can vote on English-only matters, while English MPs cannot vote on Scottish matters, as they are devolved to the Scottish Parliament. This is known as the West Lothian Question, after the late Labour MP for West Lothian, Sir Tam Dalyell. Restricting the participation of Scottish MPs could perhaps be made more workable by scheduling debate on UK issues on certain days of the week. It might also allow a proportion of MSPs to perform both roles, thereby reducing the number of politicians. Even if this proves impractical, it is certainly possible to reform Westminster's procedures to allow a better fit with the new Home Rule settlement. Equally, there would be a need to resolve disputes over jurisdiction, as well as other potential matters arising. In other countries, this would normally be done by a constitutional court. In the UK, the Supreme Court could perform this function, meaning no new body would be required.

A further area that would need to be addressed is how the Scottish government could provide input into reserved areas of policy. The Home Rule settlement outlined in this book seeks to devolve as much power as possible to the Scottish level of government, meaning there will be cases where reserved UK areas of policy overlap with Scottish areas of responsibility. The environment is one such area, with the Scottish government's domestic responsibilities overlapping with the UK government's responsibility for international relations, which involves global treaties on, for example, climate change. Another area is international trade, which despite being a UK responsibility clearly impacts the Scottish economy, prime responsibility for which rests at the Scottish level of government.

The obvious way of addressing these issues is through the existing Joint Ministerial Committee structure, which currently comprises ministers from both the UK and devolved governments. Its plenary sessions are chaired by the Prime Minister, and involve the first ministers of the devolved nations, as well as other ministers. It is governed by a memorandum of understanding, which states its role is to coordinate the relationship between the UK and the devolved nations by acting as a forum to:

- Consider non-devolved matters that affect devolved responsibilities (and vice versa).
- Consider devolved matters if it is beneficial to discuss their respective treatment in the different parts of the UK.
- Keep the arrangements for liaison between the governments under review.
- Consider disputes between the governments.

In its 2015 report entitled 'A Constitutional Crossroads: Ways Forward for the United Kingdom', the Bingham Centre for the Rule of Law set out the problems with the current arrangements, stating: 'Inter-governmental relations in the United Kingdom are characterised by informality and, to the extent to which they are regulated at all, are regulated by conventions, concordat, memorandums of understanding, and guidance notes.' The report concluded that although the memorandum of understanding had no statutory basis, it was 'based on the right sentiments but the machinery it establishes is too weak to ensure that the sentiments find their way into practice'.

One option would, therefore, be to beef up the Joint Ministerial Committee arrangements by making them part of the Home Rule constitution. Alternatively, it could be replaced by a new UK Council of Ministers. This would incorporate representatives of the component parts of the UK, including England, and is part of an envisaged quasi-federal future envisaged by MSP Murdo Fraser, who argues: 'This would ensure a better balance within a UK Council of Ministers than exists within the current JMC system, where the interests of England are not distinctly represented.'

16
Why Home Rule Now?

Home Rule is a principled and practical answer to the constitutional question facing both Scotland and the UK as a whole. It would create a new and better relationship between Scotland and the rest of the UK, based on clear principles and experience of what works well in other countries. It would clearly define the respective responsibilities of the UK and Scottish parliaments, and give people in Scotland more control over Scottish issues, while also ensuring that Scotland enjoys the benefits of being part of the wider UK. Such a settlement is, this book would argue, the best way of meeting the needs of people in Scotland. Surveys indicate this sentiment is in tune with public opinion.

The Home Rule settlement proposed here is built on three clear principles, the first of which is that there should be a presumption in favour of devolving power – the principle of subsidiarity. The proposed settlement thus restricts the powers of the UK level of government to areas that must be decided on the basis of the whole country, such as foreign affairs, defence, national security and macro-economic policy. In countries such as Canada, Australia, Germany and the USA, these are typically the responsibility of the federal level of government. Everything else becomes the responsibility of the Scottish level of government, and indeed can then be devolved further, as the process and principle of subsidiarity should not stop there.

This approach has twin benefits. On the one hand, it brings decision-making closer to the people affected, enabling the development of policy responses that specifically address Scottish (or local) priorities, opportunities or challenges. This recognises that people and communities – whether national or local – are different, and a sensible constitutional settlement will reflect this. On the other hand, it enables issues for which there can only be a single common policy to be decided at the UK level. In a world in which certain big issues can only be addressed at a global level, the clout that comes with being part of a larger entity can only serve the interests of people in Scotland.

The second principle that must underly any Home Rule settlement is that both the UK and Scottish levels of government should be responsible for raising the money that they spend in, and on behalf of, Scotland. This principle of fiscal responsibility complements the other powers that would be exercised at the Scottish level, providing the Scottish government with the necessary means to manage the economy, increase prosperity and economic opportunity, and achieve a fairer and more sustainable society.

Furthermore, fiscal responsibility increases democratic accountability. The Scottish government will be held to account for how much it spends, how it raises that money, and the effectiveness of its expenditure. This will encourage prudent spending, as the public will be fully aware of who is responsible if things go wrong. Equally, however, the UK government will be held to account for its spending in, and on behalf of, Scotland. Despite this representing a smaller proportion of overall spending under Home Rule, it is still significant and there will be every incentive to ensure this money is spent wisely, and that waste or duplication is eliminated.

The third key principle for Home Rule is that the new constitutional relationship between Scotland and the rest of the UK must be based on mutual respect. The current settlement does not achieve this, and so a new partnership of equals needs to be founded on a written constitution. This would clarify and entrench the respective powers of the UK and Scottish parliaments, and could only be changed with the consent of both parties. Similar structures have worked well in various countries across the world, demonstrating that splitting sovereignty in this way is a basis for good governance. In this regard, the benefits of Home Rule are clear: a new, stable, long-term relationship which is seen to be fair and can command the support of the vast majority of people in both Scotland and the rest of the UK.

There are alternatives to Home Rule, one of which is maintaining the status quo. This, though, assumes that the current division of powers cannot be improved upon and will always be appropriate. Such intransigence is not based on any consensus amongst the people of Scotland about the division of powers and, rather than stability, offers a recipe for further divisive conflict.

Another option is to carry on with the approach that has, in practice, been adopted since the Scottish Parliament was set up – that is, the incremental devolution of further powers as and when it has become clear there is sufficient pressure for further change. Unfortunately, this has led to ad hoc, piecemeal reform of the constitutional settlement, and represents a sticking plaster solution rather than a serious attempt at drawing up a sustainable settlement. This approach, which treats devolution as a process, is at the root of the problem.

Given the shortcomings of these options, it is this author's contention that a clear, principled alternative – to both the status quo and independence – needs to be offered to the public. The Home Rule settlement proposed in this book sets out just such an alternative.

PART 3
THE POTENTIAL OF SCOTTISH
HOME RULE

17
Introduction

A Scottish Home Rule settlement, as set out in the previous section, opens up numerous avenues for reform. Some of these – such as a new federal structure – would affect the whole of the UK, while others represent opportunities for the Scottish government in such vital areas as taxation, welfare and pensions. In this section, a variety of suggestions are put forward as to how things might be done differently under Home Rule. Of course, different people will have different views on the proposals outlined in the following chapters, and many will have alternative proposals of their own. The intention here is not to claim that these are the only – or even necessarily the best – available solutions for Scotland, but rather to shed light on the potential scope for new and innovative policy. Should Home Rule come to pass, there will inevitably be vigorous debate as to what social and economic paths should be taken. This is entirely healthy and emphasises the fundamental point that any policies implemented under Home Rule will be reflective of whichever government is elected by the people of Scotland. Post-Brexit, a debate in both Scotland and the UK is sorely needed as to where we go from here. Home Rule may prove an important catalyst for such a debate.

18
Reform of the Tax System

When asked about completing his income tax form, Albert Einstein reputedly responded: 'This is a question too difficult for a mathematician. It should be asked of a philosopher.' If we were to create an entirely new tax system, it is unlikely it would look like the one we have today – a system that over the past century has grown arms and legs and is not suited to a modern globalised world.

The beauty of Home Rule is that it gives Scotland the opportunity to radically reform the tax system. Should it choose to do so, it will inevitably get some things right – which can then be copied by other parts of the UK and even countries abroad – and some things wrong. This is the nature of change, and much can be learned from unsuccessful as well as successful attempts. One of the advantages of being a small country within a Home Rule system is that Scotland would have the freedom to try new things while still having the safety net of being part of the UK. Ultimately, it is not unreasonable to hope that the country of the Enlightenment, which produced economists of the calibre of Adam Smith, could reform the tax system in such a way as to bring it kicking and screaming into the modern world.

The ideas proposed below are not concerned with whether there should be more or less wealth redistribution, or how much the 'rich' should pay relative to the 'poor'. These are political arguments that define the traditional left vs right approach to economics, and are best determined by politicians and the ballot box. What is set out, however, is how we might create a simpler, more transparent tax system – one that is more effective in a world where capital and people can move with relative freedom across tax jurisdictions. Again, it should be emphasised that these are ideas for discussion, with the key point being that Home Rule allows for things to be done differently.

Making Tax Simpler

As mentioned earlier, the UK has now overtaken India as the country with the most extensive tax legislation in the world. Yet, essentially, over 90 per cent of all UK taxes come from three principal sources: income, goods and assets. One bold way to simplify taxation would therefore be to recognise these principal sources of tax and in doing so eliminate the plethora of other taxes that exist, such as stamp duty, inheritance tax, property transfer tax and corporation tax. In reality, these other forms of taxation raise limited amounts of revenue and simply add complications. Furthermore, the three principal forms of taxation offer more than enough scope to create whatever wealth distribution politicians may choose to promote in their manifestos.

Interestingly, businesses are not always logical in choosing jurisdictions based on tax. A company may decide to set up headquarters in a country that has low or zero corporation tax, ignoring the fact that 85 per cent of tax paid by companies is through PAYE and employers' national insurance. Corporation tax, and other taxes like it, are difficult to administer in a global world where companies can transfer profits through subsidiaries to whichever country has the lowest corporation tax rate. Similarly, wealthy individuals can dodge capital gains tax and inheritance tax by changing their residencies. Rather than just complain that this is unfair, a better solution would be to devise a simpler, more effective tax system which eliminates such loopholes.

In addition, higher-rate taxpayers in particular benefit from an array of tax relief schemes. This includes relief from pensions at the higher rate of tax, relief from charitable donations, and Enterprise Investment Scheme (EIS) relief, which returns 30 per cent of tax to investors in small companies. It seems grossly unfair that a higher-rate taxpayer receives £4,500 of tax relief on a £10,000 pension contribution, while a lower-rate taxpayer receives only £2,000. Thus, there is considerable scope not only to simplify tax, but also to simplify reliefs.

Many taxpayers, regardless of their income, would welcome a simplification of tax, including reducing the number of taxes and reliefs. To take this argument to its logical conclusion, it should be possible to construct a tax system that imposes just three principle taxes, each with the minimum number of bands and exemptions, that achieves the net effect of different taxpayers paying the same amount as they do now. The following elaborates on how this might, in theory, be made to work.

Three Principal Taxes

1. Taxes on Income

Taxes on income are principally made up of income tax, employee national insurance and employer national insurance. In the tax year 2018/19, this made up 38 per cent of total taxes in Scotland.

Currently, income tax in England, Wales and Northern Ireland has four bands: 0 per cent on the first £12,500 of salary; 20 per cent on the next £37,500; 40 per cent on the next £100,000; and 45 per cent thereafter. For earned (rather than investment) income, Scotland has five slightly different bands and rates. On top of this there is employee national insurance, which is divided into four classes, the main one being class 1. This has two bands: 12 per cent of salary up to £50,000, then 2 per cent thereafter. Then there is employers' national insurance, which is a straight 13.8 per cent on salary, paid directly by the employer rather than the employee. The above represents a very simplified explanation, as income taxes are subject to a plethora of exemptions, refinements and complications – there are, for example, income tax reliefs available for individuals making charitable donations or investing in certain small companies. Smaller companies also get threshold reliefs for employers' national insurance contributions. Given this level of complexity, it should come as no surprise that tax returns elicit so much stress.

Sometimes, there are good reasons for the intricacies of the tax system. Other times, it is the result of government attempts to raise more revenue without it being too visible to the public. In such cases, certain headline rates are left alone, and instead other taxes are created. The result has been a century of increasing tax complexity. National insurance was introduced in 1911 as a contributory scheme providing public sector cover for illness and unemployment. It was eventually expanded to provide work-related benefits, and in 1948 became, in part, compulsory. Since then, however, the direct link between national insurance and the benefits it provides has been lost, meaning it has effectively become another way to charging income tax.

Thus, one potential simplification that could be made under Home Rule would be to combine income tax, employee national insurance and employer national insurance into a single income tax. At the same time, the number of income tax reliefs could be cut. Simpler still would be to move to a flat tax rate with a fixed level of tax credit, or a citizens' income, as discussed in Chapter 19. Were this to be done, a level could be created that would have an almost identical net effect on the total aggregate levels of income tax paid at each band in the current system, but without all the complication.

This, though, would not be popular with politicians, who thrive on the complexity of the tax system. This is because it allows them to mask the overall rate of tax, and because they are reluctant to change certain emotive taxes associated with particular groups of voters. In reality, most taxpayers would prefer a simple system that allowed them to know exactly what they are paying.

2. Taxes on Goods

Taxes on goods make up around 29 per cent of Scottish revenue (excluding oil revenues). This comes mainly from value-added tax (VAT) and duties on fuel, tobacco and alcohol. Again, these taxes have expanded for historical reasons. Taxes on goods are often said to be regressive, in that they dispro-portionately affect the poor as a percentage of disposable income. While this is a political argument, and therefore something for politicians to put to the voting public, if you were looking to create a straightforward tax on sales for the modern world it is unlikely you would start with VAT.

VAT was first introduced in France in 1954 as a tax touching every stage of production. The advantage of VAT is that the end customer doesn't have to be identified, as at each stage of production VAT can be reclaimed from the previous stage. So, in theory, the end user ends up paying the VAT, as only businesses can reclaim VAT, not the customer. The problem with VAT is that, in the modern world, there are potentially a multitude of production stages, each involving different suppliers. Thus, inputs and outputs have multiplied exponentially.

For example, a van might be assembled and sold (at a price that includes VAT) by the manufacturer to a retailer. The retailer then reclaims the VAT from the manufacturer, and charges VAT to the buyer. If the buyer is a delivery van company, then it would reclaim the VAT from the retailer. However, the delivery van company then takes delivery of a load of fuel for a steel company. The steel company pays the VAT on the fuel before reclaiming it from the delivery van company. It then sells its steel to a cog manufacturer, which pays and then reclaims the VAT. The cog manufac-turer uses the steel to make a cog, which then gets sold to the van manufacturer, which in turn pays the applicable VAT, which can then be reclaimed against the sale of a van. So far, there have multiple transactions involving VAT payments and reclaims, but no net payment of VAT to the government. In other words, a huge amount of work – as any company administration department can attest to – without any revenue raised. Not only this, the system is open to error, tax avoidance and even tax evasion.

A much simpler system could be achieved if we were willing to bite the bullet and accept the need for a sales tax levied only on the end user. While this would mean identifying who the end user is, given the complexity of the current system it appears to be the lesser of two evils. In doing this, Scotland could be a first initiator in the UK of a sales tax popular in many US states.

VAT was introduced into the UK in 1973 and under EU legislation all member states are required to charge the tax within certain bands. Thus, one advantage of the UK leaving the EU is that this allows for a direct sales tax charged at the point of sale. At present, VAT in the UK is charged at 20 per cent, though again there are a plethora of exemptions – for example, children's shoes are exempt, while adult's shoes are subject to the full rate. It would be much simpler to remove these exemptions and instead have a single-rate sales tax on all services and products sold to a retail customer. This would greatly diminish the huge burden imposed on companies that have to administer VAT, as well as reduce potential losses resulting from error, tax avoidance and tax evasion.

The sales tax could be extended to duties, with a higher sales tax levied on items that have a detrimental impact on health or the environment, such as tobacco, alcohol and fuel – even sugar and plastic. Such taxes could be used to influence behaviour related to the particular social and health problems affecting Scotland.

3. Taxes on Property

Taxes on property in the UK currently consists of council tax and business rates, with council tax already devolved to local councils and, in Scotland, business rates set by the Scottish government. They raise about 10 per cent of revenues, which is relatively low compared to the amounts raised by taxes on goods and income.

Property taxes can be an effective way both of raising government revenue and making the property market work more efficiently. They are also a good means of taxing non-UK residents who benefit from having property in the UK but pay little in the way of public revenue. Again, property taxes as they currently stand are complicated and could be updated. For instance, council tax bands are based on the value of properties in 1991, as a result of which the floor of the top band is set at £325,000. This means that someone with a house valued at £325,000 pays the same amount of council tax as a person living in a £5 million mansion.

It would seem much fairer to pay a percentage of a house's current value, which could be determined every five years from the many online valuation companies, such as Zoopla. One advantage of a rebased property tax is that it would encourage efficient use of property, with, for example, parents downsizing from large houses once their children had left home.

If a government wishes to introduce greater wealth redistribution, then a relatively easy and non-regressive way to raise more in taxes is through an annual wealth tax. This would apply not only to property, but all wealth, including cash, investments and other assets (less debt).

The various proposals set out above demonstrate that by sticking to and simplifying the three principle taxes it should be possible to raise as much – if not more – revenue than is presently the case. In the process, it would also make for a more transparent and easier-to-understand system. Once again, different people will have different ideas about how best to achieve these objectives, and political considerations would need to be taken into account regarding any restructuring of Scotland's tax system. Even so, it shows how Home Rule could facilitate fundamental and coherent reform in Scotland, should the opportunity be grasped. While not every new or reformed tax will work or be popular, learning from mistakes is the only way to innovate and create a better system. Ultimately, this will provide the people of Scotland (and perhaps the rest of the UK, should it choose to take heed) with a simpler, better framework for paying for the public services they receive.

19

Ideas for Welfare Reform

Like the tax system, the welfare system that has developed over the past century or so has become fiendishly complicated for those using it, despite many of these complications being introduced in pursuit of laudable aims – such as making the system more responsive to the needs of individuals. However, as Reform Scotland's paper 'The Basic Income Guarantee' sets out, the labyrinth that is the current benefits system is clearly no longer capable of adequately serving individual users. It has become overly bureaucratic, which has added to administration costs and increased administrative errors, meaning that benefits often go unclaimed. As such, its primary objective of providing a social safety net below which people cannot fall is not being met.

The UK's welfare system has also proved ineffective in its other key task, which is to lead people back into work and away from welfare. The reason for this is the marginal rate of taxation – that is, what those moving off benefits and into work can expect to pay on each additional pound earned. In some cases, marginal tax rates can be over 90 per cent, caused by a combination of benefit withdrawal and starting to pay tax as income rises.

Recently, the UK government introduced its Universal Credit scheme both to simplify the benefits system and help people move from welfare into work. Universal Credit incorporated six previously existing benefits (Housing Benefit, Employment and Support Allowance, Jobseeker's Allowance, Child Tax Credit, Working Tax Credit, and Income Support). While this has reduced the number of benefits, there are still many others that remain, and although the marginal tax rates faced by those moving into work have been reduced, they can still be over 70 per cent in many cases.

All this leaves plenty of room for improvement. The current devolved settlement does not, however, allow Scotland to take responsibility for this, as almost all aspects of Universal Credit remain a UK responsibility. As outlined in Part 2, the Home Rule settlement proposed by this book would end this split in social security powers, instead transferring full responsibility to the Scottish government. This makes perfect sense, as it brings together important areas of policy, many aspects of which (for example, housing, health and social inclusion) are already devolved responsibilities. Similarly, working-age benefits are linked to other aspects of economic management, which are largely devolved. Thus, Home Rule would enable the adoption of coherent policies, which is essential if such deep-seated issues as social protection and the alleviation of poverty are to be addressed effectively. One of the key aims of welfare reform has always been to integrate the tax and benefits system, thereby avoiding the high marginal rates discussed above. Under Home Rule, it would be possible to explore ways of achieving this aim.

There are many potential ways of reforming welfare under Home Rule. Below, two particular avenues are examined: a citizen's basic income and a negative income tax.

Citizen's Basic Income

The citizen's basic income (CBI) goes by many different names, including basic income (BI), citizen's income (CI), universal basic income (UBI), a social dividend or a universal grant. Although there are numerous forms of CBI, the basic concept has also been supported by a variety of organisations in Scotland, including the Scottish Green Party, the Royal Society for the Encouragement of Arts, Manufactures and Commerce (RSA), and Reform Scotland. According to the Citizen's Basic Income Trust, the defining characteristics of a CBI are that it is:

- **Unconditional:** A CBI can vary with age, but there should be no other conditions. Thus, everyone of the same age receives the same CBI, irrespective of gender, employment status, family structure, contribution to society, housing costs, or any other reason.
- **Automatic:** A CBI should automatically be paid on a weekly or monthly basis.
- **Nonwithdrawable:** A CBI should not be means-tested, meaning it is unaffected by any changes in an individual's earnings or wealth.

- **Individual:** A CBI should be paid on an individual basis, rather than to a couple or household.
- **A right:** Every citizen of a country should receive a CBI. It can also be made available to resident non-citizens subject to a minimum period of legal residency.

While different CBI models offer slight variations on the above themes, the key to any CBI is that it offers a means of coordinating the income tax and benefits systems. The costs of providing the CBI would be recouped through income tax levied on all income, and by reducing means-tested benefits. Taxpayers and benefit claimants are, therefore, treated alike.

Such a system would be far simpler to understand and would involve near 100 per cent take up – as is the case with child benefit, the closest comparison in the current system. Given that the system would be cheaper to operate, errors would be reduced and it could be easily automated, providing numerous knock-on advantages. Most importantly, because a CBI is not withdrawn as a person's income rises, and is not affected by any assets, it would remove the disincentives to work associated with high marginal rates of tax.

Negative Income Tax

Another welfare reform that would become a possibility for Scotland under Home Rule would be the introduction of a negative income tax. This is an idea put forward by, amongst others, the Liberal politician Juliet Rhys-Williams and the economist Milton Friedman. Though it bears some similarities to the CBI, supporters of the respective schemes would claim they are very different.

Both policies seek to provide social assistance to those of working age on low incomes by replacing a range of benefits with a single payment. However, the key difference is that rather than a flat payment being made to everyone regardless of circumstance, a negative income tax acts as a mirror image of the existing tax system. Currently, if someone's income exceeds the allowance threshold, they pay tax on further earnings at the stipulated rate. However, if their income is below the personal allowance threshold, they simply pay no tax. With a negative income tax, if someone's income falls below the allowance threshold, the difference between the two is calculated and they receive a top-up payment. The level of top-up payment is dependent on the subsidy rate set by the government.

The simplest way to illustrate this is by setting the subsidy rate at 50 per cent and the personal allowance threshold at £12,500 (which is the 2019/20 allowance in the UK). If someone earned £0, then they would receive 50 per cent of the difference between £0 and £12,500 from the government. Thus, their total income would be £6,250. If, however, they earned £5,000, then they would receive 50 per cent of the difference between £5,000 and £12,500 from the government, meaning their total income would be £8,750. Should earnings rise to £12,500, no subsidy would be received, and above this level the individual would start paying income tax as per the current system.

Such a system would benefit from having a single form of income tax, as there are currently different thresholds for starting to pay national insurance (£8,632 in 2019/20) and income tax (£12,500 in 2019/20). The specific rates set for the negative income tax, like the CBI, would be for politicians to determine. If designed appropriately, the negative income tax would achieve many of the same benefits as the CBI in terms of integrating the tax and benefits system for those on low incomes and removing many of the disincentives to work associated with the current system. Although it is not as simple as the CBI and would require everyone to be part of the tax system, it would certainly be an improvement on the system as it stands, and would be both easier to understand and less costly to administer.

Both the CBI and the negative income tax are social assistance programmes, involving non-contributory benefits aimed at helping those of working age on low incomes. While this is the area of welfare policy that would benefit most from reform, under Home Rule there would be nothing to stop the Scottish government looking to improve other aspects of welfare policy. For example, a different approach to contributory forms of benefit might be adopted.

Furthermore, while the CBI and negative income tax would combine a number of different benefits, there are other benefits intended to deal with people's additional needs that could not be combined in this way and would need to be administered in a more personal and targeted manner. A reform programme examining how the delivery of these benefits could be improved would certainly be worthwhile.

20

A New Pensions System

Along with welfare benefits, Home Rule would transfer responsibility for pensions to the Scottish government. Some may regard this as a poisoned chalice given the problems within the system that have been building up over many years. It would be better, however, to regard this as an opportunity to introduce much-needed reform in Scotland, the aim being to create a pensions system that both meets the needs of the Scottish people and is financially sustainable in the long term.

The fundamental problems afflicting the UK pensions system are analysed in a Reform Scotland report entitled 'The Pension Guarantee', which I co-authored. Essentially, successive governments have refused to grasp the nettle of funding public pensions as it is so politically sensitive, resulting in trouble being stored up for the future.

In recent years, the UK government has introduced limited reforms – such as raising the state pension age and stipulating auto-enrolment of workers into workplace pension schemes – in an attempt to alleviate the situation. While sensible in their own right, these measures have merely scratched the surface of the problem.

The issue with the current system is that it is unfunded and that, in common with most Western countries, the UK has an ageing population. Most people assume that because they have paid their national insurance over the years the state will provide sufficiently for them in their retirement. This is a dangerous assumption, as when people pay national insurance they are not in fact paying towards the cost of their future pension. National insurance is a form of income tax and, although it goes into a fund that pays for contributory benefits, the contributions paid today are mostly used to pay today's recipients.

The potential difficulties arising from this in the future become apparent when the demographics are examined. Put simply, the pensioner-age population in the UK is forecast to grow faster than the working-age population, which means that as the cost of providing pensions goes up there will be fewer people to provide the revenue to pay for them. This is not financially sustainable. Furthermore, projections suggest that this situation will be worse in Scotland than the UK as a whole. All of this means that people today face an uncertain future, as they are reliant on whatever decisions are taken by politicians in the future, something over which they can have no foreknowledge or control.

The solution to this is to move to a funded pensions system. One way of doing this is to make it mandatory that all citizens take out fully funded, defined-contribution schemes. This is, in effect, a universal contributory pension (UCP), modelled on reforms implemented in the 1980s in Australia as described below by the politician Paul Keating:

> The point is the Labor Government in which I was Treasurer had the foresight, as far back as 1983, to see that the demographic bulge in the Australian population beginning in 2010 and rising through 2030 was a major problem, and that something substantial had to be done in dealing with it. And done early. Fortunately, the action taken since 1985–86 in increasing award then mandatory contributions to superannuation, now to a level of nine percentage points of wages, will save future generations from the budgetary stress that would otherwise have been occasioned by the sole call on the age pension system. We have at least got that far.

International comparisons show that Australia now has a highly rated pension system, with low spending on old-age pensions, high individual savings rates and growing retirement savings.

Similar benefits could be expected in Scotland. A UCP would replace national insurance, with people paying a mandatory percentage of their salary into a pension pot. This scheme would give people control over this asset, allowing it to be passed on if they died before being able to draw on it. Crucially, each generation would provide for their own retirement rather than the burden being passed to the next generation.

As with the other policy ideas presented in this section, it would be for politicians to decide on such issues as the level of the mandatory contribution. There would also, no doubt, be other ways of reforming Scotland's pensions system in pursuit of the objective of moving from an unfunded to a funded system. Regardless of the approach adopted, Home Rule provides the opportunity to institute much-needed reforms that will stand Scotland in good stead for the future.

21

Enhanced Local Democracy

As has been mentioned several times, a key principle underpinning the Home Rule settlement proposed here is subsidiarity. This principle applies just as much to the relationship between the central and local government in Scotland as it does to the relationship between Westminster and Holyrood.

A trend towards centralisation of power in Scotland has been in evidence for the past century, particularly since the Second World War. This centralisation has been driven by various different policy approaches: consolidation of local government into larger units; local government powers being transferred to quangos; reductions in councils' ability to control their own finances due to capping of local taxes; more revenue taking the form of a central grant; and funding being tied to central policy controls, directives and targets

While the establishment of the Scottish Parliament in 1999 saw democratic power flow from Westminster to Holyrood, there was no corresponding transfer of power to local government. Nor, since then, has Holyrood made any fundamental attempt to establish a new relationship with councils in Scotland. Though there have been steps forward – such as a reduction in ring-fenced funding for councils and the signing of a new concordat between central and local government – these were accompanied by a centrally imposed council tax freeze, which was then followed up by a cap on council tax increases. Thus, councils have seen a reduction in their financial autonomy.

This centralising approach has not proven to be a success. The performance of Scotland's economy and public services continues to lag behind comparable Western countries, failing in the process to adequately address longstanding issues of social disadvantage, particularly in areas such as education. There are a number of reasons for this, the most important being that Scotland is a diverse country, with different regions having different needs and priorities. Therefore, imposing uniform solutions from the centre will inevitably lead to policies that are inappropriate for many parts of Scotland, while at the same time preventing local councils from introducing the innovative policies that are needed to address local concerns and raise standards.

Some of these issues could already have been addressed by the Scottish government under its devolved powers, and it is a great pity that no administration has yet chosen to do so. In one respect, though, Home Rule provides a vital and at present unavailable catalyst for the revitalisation of local democracy.

Local Financial Responsibility

A genuine decentralisation of power means giving local communities autonomy. This includes the power to disagree with central government and do things differently if they so wish. Nineteenth-century philosopher John Stuart Mill summed this up well when he said: 'The very object of having local representation is in order that those who have any interest in common, which they do not share with the general body of their countrymen, may manage that joint interest by themselves.'

The key to such autonomy is granting councils the ability to raise their own revenue. Under Home Rule, the Scottish government would have full control over the broad range of taxes required to raise its own revenue, thereby providing the opportunity to put in place a new financial relationship with local government. This would be based on giving councils the same freedom enjoyed by the Scottish government under Home Rule – that is, the ability to raise revenue from a range of local taxes, including on property, income and sales. Together with local revenue from sales, rents, fees and charges, this would enable councils to raise the vast bulk of their own revenue. However, under this system, the Scottish government would remain responsible for administering a central grant that would ensure rural areas and areas with high levels of social deprivation were not penalised.

Enhanced fiscal responsibility for councils will increase both their autonomy and accountability, providing them with the means to do things differently and find the right balance between taxation and expenditure for their respective areas. More importantly, it would ensure that, for the most part, local people bear the financial consequences of decisions taken locally, giving councils a real incentive to provide the highest quality of service at the lowest possible cost. This will, in turn, attract people and businesses, and therefore extra revenue.

Furthermore, it would strengthen local democratic accountability. If locally elected representatives wished to do things differently – for example, to spend more on a particular area or to deal with a particular problem – then they would have to justify their spending and taxation decisions to the local electorate. This would have the added benefit of encouraging better engagement with communities about their concerns, thereby strengthening local democracy.

Reviving Local Democracy

Further things that could be done to enhance local democracy in Scotland include transferring many current quango powers to councils and instigating a review of local government structure. This should be a genuine consultation exercise that seeks to pinpoint what local people want from their councils, and may ultimately involve devolving some powers to a very local community level, as is the case in other European countries. This is in keeping with the European Commission's report, 'Effective Democracy: Reconnecting with Communities'. This states that: 'Democratic power lies with people and communities who give some of that power to governments and local governments, not the other way round.'

The usual objection to such decentralisation of power is that it will lead to a wide variation in standards and a so-called 'postcode lottery'. In response to this, Nick Clegg – then leader of the Liberal Democrats – observed in a 2008 speech to the Local Government Association:

> A postcode lottery is a terrible thing. But the terrible part of the post-code lottery isn't that things are different in different areas. The terrible part is the lottery – it's that you don't get to choose what fits you or fits your postcode. I want things to be different in different places. I want things to be different for different people. I just want people to be able to choose what suits them – not have it handed out arbitrarily by a bureaucratic lottery that no one understands.

This is the crux of the matter. Decentralisation is not a lottery or a process of chance, but a system subject to clear democratic control. Diversity of provision does not mean that services are necessarily better or worse, merely that they reflect different local needs and priorities. Even if variations in standards exist, the dynamism associated with decentralised systems is more likely to drive up standards over time.

It would certainly be appropriate if a Home Rule settlement led to the revival of local democracy in Scotland. Back in in 1995, in 'Scotland's Parliament, Scotland's Right', the Scottish Constitutional Convention declared that:

> The value of local government stems from three essential attributes:
> - First, it provides for the *dispersal of power* both to bring the reality of government nearer to the people and also to prevent the concentration of power at the centre;
> - Second, *participation*, local government is government by local communities rather than – as in the case of non-elected bodies – of local communities; and
> - Thirdly, *responsiveness*, through which it contributes to meeting local needs by delivering services.

Sadly, the importance of the above has not always been recognised in the years that followed. By giving the Scottish Parliament enhanced powers – particularly fiscal – Home Rule provides an opportunity for delegating more powers to the next level of sub-national government. For those attracted to the principles of decentralisation and the concept of subsidiarity, it is only logical that these are applied to local government.

22

Towards a Federal UK

Scottish Home Rule refers very specifically to the relationship between Scotland and the rest of the UK. This bilateral relationship would, as far as possible, work within the UK's existing institutions of governance, thereby introducing minimal disruption to their proceedings. While one of the key features of Scottish Home Rule is that it would not affect the relationships between the other devolved nations and the UK, once it was up and running, and its benefits apparent, it is perfectly possible that Wales and Northern Ireland may want their own Home Rule settlements. This is entirely reasonable and the system should be flexible enough to cope with this.

Over the past couple of years, federalism has increasingly been the subject of discussion by political think tanks. The Constitutional Reform Group was set up in 2015 in order to give voice to the debate for a new Act of Union, and in October of that year introduced a House of Commons private members bill called 'An Act of Union Bill'. The Federal Union, formed in 1938, is calling for a codified federalist constitution for the UK, while Professor Jim Gallagher, a former civil servant, produced a paper for the The Fabian Society in August 2019 entitled 'Progressive Federalism'. These are just some examples of how current political thought is solidifying on this topic.

A Home Rule settlement for Northern Ireland or Wales would not need to mirror that of Scotland's. Instead, it would be important that any such settlement negotiated between the respective devolved countries and the UK government reflected their particular needs, priorities and histories. For example, the fact that a single legal jurisdiction for England and Wales existed prior to the establishment of the Welsh Assembly is an obvious difference to the situation in Scotland. Such differences are reflected in the current devolved settlements seen in Scotland, Wales and Northern Ireland. Although all three share similar structures, there is no consistent division between devolved and reserved matters.

It would, therefore, be relatively straightforward to move to a system of asymmetric Home Rule, in which the various parts of the UK had different responsibilities and different relationships with Westminster. This would be similar to Spain and its relationship with its different regions. Such a change could largely be achieved using existing institutions. However, moving to a fully federal system, whether asymmetric or symmetric, would require more fundamental change to the UK's constitution. Although there is no immediate prospect of this, it should not be ruled out as a possibility for the future. In this respect, Scottish Home Rule could well be a precursor to a fully federal UK, and so it is worth examining the types of changes that would be needed to achieve a federal structure.

Federal Constitution

Scottish Home Rule would require a written constitution setting out the new relationship between the UK and Scotland. Similarly, a federal system would require a new written constitution setting out the relationship between all the constituent parts of the United Kingdom, including which powers were reserved to Westminster. In a symmetrical federal system, such as that used in the USA or Australia, these central UK responsibilities would need to be consistent. This, though, would not be the case in an asymmetrical system. While such systems can work, they do introduce a greater level of complexity into the constitutional relationship. Thus, if the UK does decide to move towards federalism, it would be better to do so on the basis of a symmetrical system. In such a system, the powers of the UK or federal level of government would be similar to those set out for Scottish Home Rule previously in Chapter 7 – that is, international relations, defence, monetary policy currency, etc. Anything not set out in the constitution as a UK-level responsibility would automatically become the responsibility of the sub-national level of government.

Governance of England

Within a federal UK, Scotland, Wales and Northern Ireland would be governed by their existing parliaments or assemblies, which would have their constitutional powers formalised in the new constitutional arrangements. This leaves England as the only constituent part of the UK without its own legislature, with the House of Commons currently doubling as a parliament for both the UK and England.

One option would simply be to make these two roles more clear-cut. This would mean the House of Commons functioning separately as a UK Parliament legislating for the whole country – including representation from the whole of the UK – and as an English Parliament legislating purely on English matters and consisting only of English MPs. Practically, this could be done by allocating Monday and Tuesday to UK matters, with all MPs attending, while for the rest of the week Westminster would legislate solely on English matters, meaning only English MPs were required. Under this model, the House of Lords would continue its present role of scrutinising legislation, whether English-only or UK-wide. Of course, this option begs the question of what Scottish, Welsh and Northern Irish MPs would do Wednesday to Friday, given that devolved business would be dealt with by members of their own parliaments.

A second option would be to create a new English Parliament. This could be done in an entirely separate building from the House of Commons, with separately elected MEPs. In this scenario, it would make sense to reduce the total number of UK MPs, given the reduced amount of UK-specific legislation that would need to be passed once England had its own parliament. The House of Lords could either become a second chamber for purely UK legislation, or could be the second chamber for all the parliaments.

A third option would be to divide England into federal regions – for example, London and the South-east, Manchester, Midlands, Yorkshire – and for regional parliaments to be set up across the country. These would have the same powers as the equivalent bodies in Scotland, Wales and Northern Ireland. This would be a subject for people in England to decide upon, with people in other parts of the UK having no say in the matter.

UK Federal Parliament

Whichever governance option was chosen by people in England, some form of new federal UK Parliament would be needed to decide UK-wide issues. At present, around a fifth of Westminster legislative time is spent on UK-wide matters. Therefore, given the reduced time commitment, it would not be necessary to maintain the current number of House of Commons or House of Lords members to handle purely UK matters. The form of the UK federal system would need to be debated and decided at its inception. Such a debate would need to take into account substantial anecdotal evidence that the public has lost trust in politicians and the current structure of government. Results from the British Social Attitudes survey show that in 1986, 36 per cent of people polled trusted governments to place the needs of the nation above the interests of their own political party. By 2007, this had fallen to 18 per cent. Thus, a move to a federal system could provide a good opportunity to conduct a major review into how the current political system is structured. This process could at the very least debate, and even potentially address, such issues as an outdated House of Lords, proportional representation, the lack of a second chamber in devolved governments, and whether there should be a directly elected Prime Minister.

Three federal structures that might form the basis of such a debate are:

1. A reduced number of UK MPs (probably no more than 150) are voted in separately from England, Scotland, Wales and Northern Ireland to deal purely with UK matters. This could involve a form of proportional representation in order to more accurately reflect party voting and end the current situation where, in many constituencies, voting for a particular party effectively has no impact on that party's success. Similarly, were the House of Lords to become a second chamber for purely UK legislation, then it too should see a reduction in members. The UK Prime Minister would be appointed and Cabinet formed from the party or parties capable of demonstrating that they had enough support to form a government.

2. A limited number of English, Scottish, Welsh and Northern Irish MPs from their own parliaments are allocated on a party basis to spend part of the week in the UK Parliament dealing with UK-wide issues. For instance, 60 MSPs (out of the current 129), chosen to reflect the party balance at Holyrood, would spend a day a week at Westminster on purely UK matters. Similarly, in recognition of its larger size, England would have 500 MPs in the UK Parliament. The House of Lords could then become a second chamber for both the UK and the English, Scottish, Welsh and Northern Irish parliaments. Again, the UK Prime Minister would be appointed and Cabinet formed from the party or parties demonstrating sufficient support to form a government.

3. A new system is created to replace both the Commons and Lords. This could be modelled on another federal system, such as that used in the USA, with the House of Lords converted into a Senate and the House of Commons converted into a House of Representatives. Similar to the role played by the US Senate, a UK Senate would represent the constituent parts of the UK equally. In the USA, two senators are elected for each of the 50 states, meaning larger states – such as California – cannot dominate smaller ones, such as Rhode Island. The UK House of Representatives, by contrast, would reflect the relative populations of England, Scotland, Wales and Northern Ireland. The Prime Minister could also become an elected executive post, with a straight first-past-the-post election across the UK. The numbers in both new houses could be reduced to reflect the diminished number of responsibilities remaining at the UK level.

Constitutional Court

Federal systems throw up disputes regarding whether a particular issue falls under the jurisdiction of the federal government or to the governing body of one of the federation's constituent parts. This is usually decided by a constitutional court, meaning that in the UK this role could be performed by the Supreme Court. No new body would then be required.

Constitutional Convention

If the countries of the UK do decide to move towards a fully federal system, then they will need a body in which to discuss the framing of the new constitution. The history of Scottish Home Rule demonstrates that a constitutional convention is a good way of discussing and deciding such issues. The make-up of such a body would need to be carefully considered and, as with the UK House of Representatives outlined above, all the UK's constituent parts would require equal representation. This would involve Scotland, England, Wales and Northern Ireland sending the same number of delegates, though how these were chosen would be up to each of the countries to decide.

A move to a fully federal system would provide real clarity about the roles and responsibilities of the various parliaments and assemblies in the UK. Additionally, assuming a symmetrical form of federalism was chosen, the constituent parts of the UK would all be treated equally, thereby reducing potential resentment. Countries that have followed this path, such as Australia and the USA, have demonstrated that it is a sustainable and successful model to follow.

Of course, a fully federal system may not be deemed the right model for the UK, and even if it was, it would inevitably take a long time to agree a new federal constitution. This is why Home Rule represents the best option in the short term, offering as it does many of the benefits of federalism without the upheaval a federal system would entail.

Conclusion

How would you know whether Scotland had achieved Home Rule as set out in this book? This is a good question, and can be looked at from the perspectives of both independence and unionism.

On the one hand, Home Rule is differentiated from independence in that the people of Scotland would have to accept that, on UK matters, they are represented as UK citizens rather than as Scots. Thus, Scotland would not have any special veto over a defence issue, just as Florida cannot veto Congress launching a foreign invasion. On the other hand, Home Rule is differentiated from unionism in that the people of Scotland would know control over domestic matters is decided solely by them, and that this cannot be unilaterally overruled by Westminster and its Prime Minister.

As we have recently learnt from painful experience in the UK, referendums tend to be more about emotions than expert analysis. The problem with having a dichotic choice, particularly in the event of a close result, is that the emotional undercurrent remains unresolved. This can clearly be seen in the case of the Brexit referendum and its aftermath. Meanwhile, a second referendum on independence remains a major source of controversy in Scotland. Following the Brexit vote, it is inevitable the SNP will seek to secure one in the next few years. To hold a legal referendum, the Scottish First Minister needs the UK Prime Minister to grant a Section 30 order. Thus far, Boris Johnson has shown little inclination to do so, continuing in the footsteps of his predecessor, Theresa May. In the wake of the Conservatives' 2019 general election victory, this is unlikely to change in the near future.

However, the next Scottish Parliament elections are due in May 2021. If the SNP and Scottish Greens include a commitment to another independence referendum in their manifestos and command a majority in the new parliament, then many believe this constitutes a renewed mandate for a referendum. Though the Johnson government may see things differently, it certainly cannot be ruled out that another referendum will take place in the next few years. Should this happen, Home Rule needs to be one of the constitutional options on the table. The referendum would thus offer three options – the status quo, home rule or independence – with a two-question format required to come to the decision. This was exactly what was proposed by Alex Salmond in 2014, before being rejected by David Cameron. In the event of another referendum, it remains the best way of achieving an outcome that will provide an emotional release for both sides of the debate. Another single-question referendum offering only independence or the current constitutional settlement is likely to lead to another narrow result one way or the other. This will simply lead to further division and rancour.

Even if no independence referendum takes place, Home Rule remains the best way of bringing about a stable, long-term constitutional settlement that meets the needs of both Scotland and the UK as a whole. If you as a reader believe in Home Rule, or even just that it should be an option for the people of Scotland, the question remains of how you would influence this debate. There are essentially two ways. The first is though civic society, which has long played a role in political debate within Scotland. Communities, churches, trade unions, trade bodies – as well as the many other organisations and groups that make up Scottish society – have the power to lobby both the UK and Scottish governments regarding their members' interests.

The second is through the political parties themselves. While the Liberal Democrats have traditionally been the party that has offered explicit support for Home Rule, many across the political spectrum regard Home Rule as the best option. You can therefore influence your local politicians and whichever party or parties you support to promote this option in a referendum. Ultimately, what is needed is a genuine cross-party movement arguing the case for Home Rule as the best answer to Scotland's constitutional question. Only when a broad consensus for such a settlement has been reached is it likely that the UK government will be persuaded to adopt such a policy.

Bibliography

BBC News [website] (2015), 'Yanis Varoufakis: In His Own Words'. www.bbc.co.uk/news/business-31111905

BBC News [website] (2017), 'Who is Nicola Sturgeon? A Profile of the SNP Leader'. www.bbc.co.uk/news/uk-scotland-25333635

BBC News [website] (2018), 'Political Heroes: Nicola Sturgeon on Winnie Ewing'. www.bbc.co.uk/news/uk-politics-43343426

Bingham Centre for the Rule of Law (2015), 'A Constitutional Crossroads: Ways Forward for the United Kingdom'. www.biicl.org/documents/595_a_constitutional_crossroads. pdf?showdocument=1

Citizen's Basic Income Trust (n.d.), 'What Is It? A Citizen's Basic Income is an Unconditional Income for Every Citizen' [webpage]. https://citizensincome.org/citizens-income/what-is-it/

Commission on Scottish Devolution (2009), 'Serving Scotland Better: Scotland and the United Kingdom in the 21st Century'. http://news.bbc.co.uk/1/shared/bsp/hi/pdfs/15_06_09_calman.pdf

Commission on Strengthening Local Democracy (2014), 'Effective Democracy: Reconnecting with Communities'.

Davidson, Jenni (2016), 'Profile: Donald Dewar the Architect of the Scottish Parliament', *Holyrood Magazine*, 21 July. www.holyrood.com/articles/inside-politics/profile-donald-dewar-architect-scottish-parliament

Duclos, Nathalie (2017), 'The 1970s: A "Paradoxical Decade" for the Scottish National Party', *French Journal of British Studies*, XXII – Hors série. https://journals.openedition.org/rfcb/1712

Edinburgh Evening News (2019), 'Scotland's 1979 Devolution Plans: 40 Years On From the "Yes" Vote that Wasn't', 1 March. www.edinburghnews.scotsman.com/education/scotland-s-1979-devolution-plans-40-years-on-from-the-yes-vote-that-wasn-t-1-4881420

Elrick, Mike (2014), 'John Smith – Labour's Lost Leader', *Scotsman*, 27 April.

Ewing, Winifred (1998), 'Obituary: Dr Robert McIntyre', *Independent*, 4 February. www.independent.co.uk/news/obituaries/obituary-dr-robert-mcintyre-1142811.html

Fraser Murdo (2019), 'Our Still United Kingdom: A "Quasi-Federal" Future?', Bright Blue [blog article]. https://brightblue.org.uk/quasi-federal-future/#_ftn18

Gallagher, Jim (2019), 'Progressive Federalism', The Fabian Society

Gordon, Mike (2015), 'The Permanence of Devolution: Parliamentary Sovereignty and Referendum Requirements', Scottish Constitutional Futures Forum [blog article]. www.scottishconstitutionalfutures.org/Opinionand Analysis/ViewBlog

Post/tabid/1767/articleType/ArticleView/articleId/6113/Mike-Gordon-The-Permanence-of-Devolution-Parliamentary-Sovereignty-and-Referendum-Require ments.aspx

Guardian (2007), 'Obituary: Lord Ewing', 11 June. www.theguardian.com/news/2007/jun/11/guardianobituaries.scotland

Hallett, Andrew Hughes and Drew Scott (2010), 'Scotland: A New Fiscal Settlement', Centre for Dynamic Macroeconomic Analysis. www.st-andrews.ac.uk/CDMA/ papers/wp1009.pdf

Hallwood, Paul and Ronald MacDonald (2009), *The Political Economy of Financing Scottish Government: Considering a New Constitutional Settlement for Scotland*, Edward Elgar.

Herald (1993), 'A Salute to Scotland's Standard Bearer', 10 April. www.heraldscotland.com/news/12574157.a-salute-to-scotlands-standard-bearer/

Igoe, Brian (2013), 'Daniel O'Connell's Childhood', The Irish Story [website]. www.theirishstory.com/2013/02/03/daniel-oconnells-childhood/#.Xq2sYqhKiUm

IPPR (2013), 'Funding Devo More: Fiscal Options for Strengthening the Union'. www.ippr.org/files/images/media/files/publication/2013/01/funding-devo-more_Jan2013_10210.pdf

IPPR (2014), 'Devo More and Welfare: Devolving Benefits and Policy for a Stronger Union'. www.ippr.org/files/images/media/files/publication/ 2014/03/Devo-more-and-welfare_Mar2014_11993.pdf

Kane, Nathan (2015), 'A Study of the Debate on Scottish Home Rule 1886–1914', PhD thesis, University of Edinburgh. www.era.lib.ed.ac.uk/bitstream/handle/1842/25752/Kane2015.pdf?sequence=2&isAllowed=y

Keating, Paul (2007), 'The Story of Modern Superannuation', address to Australian Pensions and Investment Summit, 31 October. www.keating.org.au/shop/item/the-story-of-modern-superannuation-31-october-2007

Lloyd-Jones, Naomi (2014), 'A Separate Scotland', *History Today*, volume 64, issue 8. www.historytoday.com/archive/separate-scotland

MacKay, Donald (ed.) (2011), 'Scotland's Economic Future', Reform Scotland. https://reformscotland.com/wp-content/uploads/2011/10/scotlands economicfuture.pdf

McNamara, Robert (2019), 'Charles Stewart Parnell', ThoughtCo. [website]. www.thoughtco.com/charles-stewart-parnell-1773852

McNamara, Robert (2019), 'Daniel O'Connell of Ireland, The Liberator', ThoughtCo. [website]. www.thoughtco.com/daniel-oconnell-of-ireland-the-liberator-1773858

Morrogh, Michael (2001), 'Mr Gladstone and Ireland', *History Today*, issue 39. www.historytoday.com/archive/mr-gladstone-and-ireland

Reform Scotland (2008), 'Fiscal Powers'. https://reformscotland.com/wp-content/uploads/2008/11/fiscal_powers.pdf

Reform Scotland (2009), 'Fiscal Powers: 2nd Edition'. https://reformscotland.com/wp-content/uploads/2009/10/fiscal_powers_2nd_edition.pdf

Reform Scotland (2011), 'Devolution Plus'. https://reformscotland.com/wp-content/uploads/2011/09/Devolution_plus2.pdf

Reform Scotland (2014), 'The Pension Guarantee'. https://reformscotland.com/wp-content/uploads/2014/02/ The_Pension_Guarantee.pdf

Reform Scotland (2016), 'The Basic Income Guarantee'. https://reformscotland.com/
wp-content/uploads/2016/02/The-Basic-Income-Guarantee-1.pdf

Roy, Kenneth (2011), 'King John and the Headstone in the Corner', Newsnet.scot
[website]. https://newsnet.scot/archive/king-john-and-the-headstone-in-the-
corner/

Scotsman (2017), 'Obituary: Canon Kenyon Wright, Campaigner for Scottish
Devolution', 27 January. www.scotsman.com/news/obituaries/obituary-canon-
kenyon-wright-campaigner-for-scottish-devolution-1-4350129

Scottish Conservatives (2014), 'Commission on the Future Governance of Scotland'.
www.scottishconservatives.com/wordpress/wp-content/uploads/2014/06/
Strathclyde_Commission_14.pdf

Scottish Constitutional Convention (1995), 'Scotland's Parliament, Scotland's Right'.

Scottish Government (2014), 'More Powers for the Scottish Parliament: Scottish
Government Proposals'. www.webarchive.org.uk/wayback/archive/
20170701141846mp_/http://www.gov.scot/Resource/0046/00460563.pdf

Scottish Green Party (2014), 'Scottish Green Party submission to Smith Commission
on Devolution'. https://webarchive.nationalarchives. gov.uk/20151202171105/
http://www.smith-commission.scot/resources/ political-party-proposals/

Scottish Labour's Devolution Committee (2014), 'Powers for a Purpose:
Strengthening Accountability and Empowering People'.
https://b.3cdn.net/scotlab/277fe5eb9b114b9a3c_1pm6iir9r.pdf

Scottish Liberal Democrats (2012), 'Federalism: The Best Future for Scotland'.
http://worldofstuart.excellentcontent.com/repository/FederalismBestFuture.pdf

Scottish Liberal Democrats (2014), 'Campbell II: The Second Report of the Home
Rule and Community Rule Commission'.
http://worldofstuart.excellentcontent.com/repository/CampbellIIreport.pdf

SPICe (2015), 'The Smith Commission Report: Overview'. www.parliament.scot/
ResearchBriefingsAndFactsheets/S4/SB_15-03_The_Smith_Commission_
Report-Overview.pdf

Steel Commission (2006), 'Moving to Federalism – A New Settlement for Scotland'.
https://web.archive.org/web/20131113121108/http:// www.scotlibdems.org.uk/
files/steelcommission.pdf

Tench, Alan (2014), 'Devo More: The Path to a Federal UK, Not Ever Looser
Union', *Juncture Online*, IPPR [website]. www.ippr.org/juncture/devo-more-the-
path-to-a-federal-uk-not-ever-looser-union

Tomkins, Adam (2016), 'Shared Rule: What Scotland Needs to Learn from
Federalism', Reform Scotland. https://reformscotland.com/wp-content/
uploads/2016/04/Shared-Rule.pdf

Torrance, David (2019), 'Reserved Matters in the United Kingdom', House of
Commons Library briefing paper. https://commonslibrary.parliament.uk/
research-briefings/cbp-8544/

All websites last accessed 6 May 2020.

Appendices

Appendix I
Summary of UK Parliament Powers Under a Home Rule Settlement

General Reservations:

- Constitution (Crown, Union, UK Parliament)
- Registration and funding of UK political parties
- International relations
- International development
- Regulation of international trade
- UK civil service
- Defence
- Treason

Specific Reservations:

Head A. Financial and Economic Matters
- Fiscal policy (power to raise and collect taxes in Scotland to meet UK expenditure in, and on behalf of, Scotland and administer a redistribution fund)
- Economic policy (ensuring UK single market operates effectively, with free movement of goods, services, capital and people based on principle of mutual recognition)
- Monetary policy (macro-economic management, including growth and stability fund)
- Currency

Head B. Home Affairs
- UK elections
- Immigration and nationality
- National security, official secrets and terrorism
- Emergency powers
- Extradition
- Access to non-Scottish public bodies

Head L. Miscellaneous
- Control of nuclear, biological and chemical weapons and other weapons of mass destruction
- Time
- Outer space
- Antarctica

Appendix II
Summary of Current Scottish Parliament Powers

- Abortion
- Agriculture, forestry and fisheries (excluding EU powers)
- Air weapons
- Consumer advocacy and advice
- Crown estate in Scotland
- Culture and creative industries
- Economic development
- Education and training
- Employment programmes
- Energy efficiency and fuel poverty schemes
- Environment and planning
- Fire services
- Fiscal powers (income tax including setting rates and thresholds; air passenger duty; aggregates levy; stamp duty land tax; landfill tax; partial assignment of vat; borrowing powers up to £2.2 billion for capital spending and £500 million for revenue spending)
- Gaming machine licensing powers (specifically to control the number of fixed-odds betting terminals)
- Health and social services
- Housing
- Justice
- Local government and local government elections (including franchise)
- Onshore oil and gas licensing
- Scottish Parliament elections
- Social security (control over certain benefits outside of Universal Credit and the power to vary the housing element of Universal Credit and to vary payment arrangements)
- Social work
- Sport
- Tourism
- Transport (including road signs; drink-driving alcohol limits; speed limits and functions of the British Transport Police. Excluding most power over aviation and shipping)

Appendix III
Summary of New Scottish Parliament Powers Under a Home Rule Settlement

General Reservations:

- Responsibility for the existence of the High Court of Justiciary and the Court of Session
- Registration and funding of Scottish political parties
- Scottish civil service

Specific Reservations:

Head A. Financial and Economic Matters (power to raise taxes and borrow, within limits, to meet Scottish expenditure; financial services; financial markets; money laundering)

Head B. Home Affairs (misuse of drugs; data protection and access to information; firearms; entertainment; scientific procedures on live animals; betting, gaming and lotteries; lieutenancies)

Head C. Trade and Industry (business associations; insolvency; competition; intellectual property; import and export control; sea fishing outside the Scottish zone; consumer protection; product standards; safety and liability; weights and measures; telecommunications; postal services; research councils; designation of assisted areas; industrial development; protection of trading and economic interests)

Head D. Energy (electricity; oil; gas; coal; nuclear energy; energy conservation)

Head E. Transport (road, marine and air transport)

Head F. Social Security (non-devolved social security schemes; child support; pensions)

Head G. Regulation of the Professions (architects, health professions and auditors)

Head H. Employment (employment and industrial relations; health and safety; non-devolved job search and support)

Head J. Health and Medicines (xenotransplantation; embryology; surrogacy and genetics; medicines; medical supplies and poisons; welfare foods)

Head K. Media and Culture (broadcasting; public lending right; government indemnity scheme and property accepted in satisfaction of tax)

Head L. Miscellaneous (judicial remuneration; equal opportunities; Ordnance Survey)

Index

Abortion Act (1967) 47
Act of Union (1707) 32–33
Act of Union (1801) 28–29
Act of Union Bill (2015) 156
Action of Churches Together in Scotland
 (*see also* Scottish Council of
 Churches) 46
agricultural depression 31
Alexander, Wendy 49
Antarctica, policy on 101
Arab-Israeli War (1973) 44

Bank Charter Act (1844–45) 89
Barnett Formula 52, 57, 124
Bentham, Jeremy 28
Bingham Centre for the Rule of Law 132
Brand, Jack 46
Brexit Party 73
Brexit referendum (2016) 18, 72–3, 162
British Board of Film Classification 90
British Social Attitudes survey 159
Brown, Gordon 14, 48, 63, 69
Buchanan-Smith, Alick 44

Callaghan, James 44, 48
Calman, Sir Kenneth 55
Calman Commission 13, 55, 57, 61–2
Cameron, David 9, 13–14, 20, 57, 62, 65,
 72, 163
Campaign for a Scottish Assembly 46
Campaign for Fiscal Responsibility 123
Campaign for Nationalism in Scotland 60
Campaign for Scottish Home Rule
 69–70, 82, 102, 130
 guiding principles 14, 69–70
Campbell, Gordon 42
Campbell, John 12

Campbell, Menzies 9–10
care homes, responsibility for 91
Catholic Relief Act (1791) 27
central government grants 109
Chamberlain, Joseph 32
Channel Islands, tax system in 113
Choosing Scotland's Future 55
Church of England 27
Church of Ireland 27, 31
Church of Scotland 48
Citizen's Basic Income Trust 147
civil service, responsibility for 85
Claim of Right for Scotland (1988) 9, 46
Clarke, Gavin 36
Clegg, Nick 65, 154
Commission on Scottish Devolution 55
communities, autonomy for 153
Constitutional Crossroads, A (report) 132
Constitutional Reform Group 156
Convention of the Royal Burghs 35
Cook, Robin 48
Corbyn, Jeremy 73
Creative Scotland 12
Crofters Party 36
Cowan, Sir William H. 36
Cunningham, George 45
Cunningham, Roseanna 59
currency, choice of 21, 111–2, 120

Daily Record 63
Dalyell, Tam 131
data protection, responsibility for 90
Davidson, Ruth 72
Davies, Ron 17
decentralisation, calls for 19, 25, 74, 116,
 153–5
Declaration of Arbroath (1320) 46

Declaration of Perth (1968) 43
defence, responsibility for 85–6
Department of Work and Pensions (DWP) 67
Designated Area Migration Agreements (DAMAs) 92
Devo Max 20, 57, 61–2
Devo Plus Group 13, 58
Devolution Plus report 13, 58
devolution referendums – *see* referendums
Dewar, Donald 17, 48–49
divided sovereignty, concept of 79, 81
Driver and Vehicle Licensing Agency (DVLA) 96
Duclos, Nathalie 42–45

Easter Rising (1916) 36
economic policy, responsibility for 88–9
economic stability, importance of 123
Edinburgh Agreement (2012) 13–14, 18, 20, 62
Einstein, Albert 140
Electoral Commission 62
Elrick, Mike 49
employment policy, responsibility for 98
energy policy, responsibility for 95–6
Enterprise Investment Schemes 141
equal opportunities policy, responsibility for 100
Equality Acts (2006, 2010) 100
Erskine of Mar, Ruaraidh 38
European Exchange Rate Mechanism 120
European Union 21
Ewing, Harry 47
Ewing, Margaret 61
Ewing, Winifred 38, 41–3, 60

Fabian Society 156
Progressive Federalism paper 156
Farage, Nigel 73
farming, responsibility for 91
federal framework, calls for 14–15, 19, 22, 25, 53, 58, 78, 84, 131, 134, 156–61
federal nations 19, 81, 86, 107, 119, 160
Federal Parliaments, proposals for 158–60

federalism
  difference from Home Rule 17, 19; fiscal 54; in the EU 111
Fenian Rising (1867) 31
Fenians 29
Financial Services Advisory Board 12
fiscal federalism 54
fiscal policy 106–17
  breakdown of 103–4; importance of 102; responsibility for 54–8, 87–8, 98, 107; spending matching income 114; with UK government 108
Fiscal Settlement for Scotland 53–54, 118–9, 128
Franklin, Benjamin 111
Fraser, Murdo 57, 133
French Finance Bill (2013) 106
French Revolution 27
Fresh Talent scheme 92
Friedman, Milton 148
Fry, Michael 45, 57

Gallagher, Professor Jim 156
Gibb, Professor Dewar 38, 40
Gillies, William 38
giving councils tax-raising powers 153
Gladstone, William Ewart 29–33, 35–36
  failure with Home Rule Bills 31; supporting Home Rule in Ireland 31
Glasgow Govan by-election (1973) 43
Glasgow Govan by-election (1988) 50
Glasgow University Scottish Nationalist Association 38
Gordon, Mike 71
Government of Scotland Bill (1914) 36, 77
Graham, Robert Cunninghame 33–34
Greece, recession in 120–22
Green Party 48, 147, 162
Grieve, Sir Robert 46

Hallett, Andrew Hughes 56
Hallwood, Paul 57
Hamilton by-election (1967) 41–43
Hardie, Keir 33
health, responsibility for 99
Heath, Edward 43
Highland Land League 35, 38

HMRC 106, 119
Holtham Commission 124
Home, Lord 45
home affairs, responsibility for 90
'Home Rule all Round' campaign 34
Home Rule
    concept of 17–18, 77, 134;
    decentralising 19, 25, 74, 116, 152–5;
    devolution of powers 80; difference
    from federalism 17, 19; difference
    from independence 77, 162;
    difference from unionism 162;
    division of powers in 82–101, 134;
    financing of 102; fiscal settlement
    for 118; partnership of equals 18;
    principles of 14, 70, 102, 118, 130,
    134–5, 152; split sovereignty 79,
    81
Home Rule for Ireland Bills (1886, 1893)
    29, 31–33, 35
Home Rule League (previously Irish
    Home Government Association) 29

Iceland, recession in 120–22
Igoe, Brian 27
immigration, responsibility for 91
independence
    debates on 13, 20–21, 61–5; distinct
    from Home Rule 17–18, 26, 37, 39,
    77–9, 122, 162–3; movement 25, 38,
    41, 77–8; referendums on 14–15, 18,
    20–21, 58–65, 71–3, 162–3; support
    for 44–5, 52, 80
Independent Labour Party (ILP) 37, 48
Institute for Public Policy Research 58
International relations, division of power
    in 84
International trade, policy for 132
Irish Catholic Association 28
Irish Home Government Association
    (later Home Rule League) 29
Irish Home Rule movement 27–36
    electoral success 30
Irish Land Acts (1870, 1881) 31
Irish Parliamentary Party 30, 32
Irish Republican Brotherhood 29
Isle of Man, tax system in 113
It's Scotland's Oil campaign 43–44

Johnson, Boris 18, 73, 162
Johnston, Russell 9
Johnston, Tom 37

Kane, Nathan 34–35
Keating, Paul 151
Kennedy, Charles 9
Kerevan, George 33
Kierkegaard, Søren 25
Kilbrandon Report 43
Kilmainham Treaty 30
Kinnock, Neil 106

Land Act (1881) 30–31
Leonard, Richard 73
Liberal Democrat Party
    Community Rule Commission report
    63
Lib-Lab Pact (1977) 47
Lloyd-Jones, Naomi 33–35
local democracy, enhancement of
    154–5
Local Government Association 154

MacAskill, Kenny 59–60
McConnell, Jack (now Lord) 12, 92
MacCormick, John 9, 37–39, 78
MacCormick, Neil 40
MacDonald, Margo 43, 59, 71
MacDonald, Ramsay 33
MacDonald, Ronald 57
McIntyre, Robert 40–41
MacKay, Sir Donald 78
Mackintosh, John 44
McNamara, Robert 27, 29
Maritime and Coastguard Agency 96
Mawdsley, Geoff 12
Maxton, John 48
May, Theresa 18, 72–3, 162
media and culture, responsibility for 99
Meek, Brian 45
Miliband, Ed 65
Mill, John Stuart 153
Moore, Michel 9, 62
Morrogh, Michael 31
Morton, Graham 33
Motherwell by-election (1945) 40
Muirhead, Roland 37–38

National Association for the Vindication of Scottish Rights 33
National Conversation 55, 61
National Galleries of Scotland 12
national insurance 149
National Land League 30
National Party of Scotland 34
national security, responsibility for 93
nationalism 25, 33, 60, 73–4
negative income tax 148–9

O'Connell, Daniel 27–29
Office of Rail Regulation 96
Ordnance Survey 100
O'Shea, Katherine 30

Paine, Thomas 28
Parnell, Charles Stewart 29–32
Peel, Sir Robert 28
'Penny for Scotland' proposal 61
pensions systems
    funded 151; Pension Guarantee 150;
    state 67, 97–8, 126, 150
personal allowance threshold 149
Plaid Cymru 43, 60
political parties, division of power in 83
Poll Tax, introduction of 61, 106
Project Fear 63
public spending deficit
    borrowing to cover 126; increased
    taxes to cover 127; reducing
    expenditure to cover 12; ways of
    addressing 125
Purvis, Jeremy 13

recessions in Greece and Iceland 120–22
referendum on devolution (1979) 26, 40,
    45, 48, 50, 60, 78
referendum on devolution (1997) 45,
    49–50, 52–7, 61, 78
referendum on EU membership (2016)
    18, 72, 162
referendum on independence (2014)
    13–15, 18–21, 59–65, 71, 78, 162–3
    debates on 63; Edinburgh Agreement
    13–14, 18, 20, 62; framing the
    question 62
Referendums (Scotland) Bill (2019) 73

Reform Act (1832) 35
Reform Scotland 12, 15, 57, 78, 146–7,
    150
    Basic Income Guarantee paper 146
    Scotland's Economic Future paper 78
    The Pensions Guarantee paper 150
Regulated Social Fund 68
Repeal Association 28
Research and development, responsibility
    for 91
research councils, future of 95
Revenue Scotland 56
Rhys-Williams, Juliet 148
Rifkind, Malcolm 44
Roman Catholic Relief Act (1829) 28
Romans, John 34
Rosebery, Lord 35
Rousseau, Jean-Jacques 28
Roy, Kenneth 38–40
Royal Commission on the Constitution
    (1969) 43
Royal Society 147

Salmond, Alex 12–13, 20, 59–62, 66, 78,
    92, 163
    banned from Commons 61; member
    of 79 Group 59; gradualist approach
    to independence 61; leader of SNP
    61; MP for Banff and Buchan 60;
    resigning as leader 71; trial 73
Scotland Act (1978) 9, 44–45
Scotland Act (1998) 9, 49–52, 55, 70, 80,
    130
Scotland Act (2012) 55–56, 62–3, 104
Scotland Act (2016) 70, 97, 104, 130
Scotland and Wales Bill (1976) 44
Scotland's Future (SNP manifesto) 62
Scotland's Parliament; Scotalnd's Right 155
Scots National League 38
Scott, Drew 56
Scottish Assembly, proposals for 44
Scottish Constitutional Convention
    47–50, 155
Scottish Constitutional Futures Forum
    71
Scottish Convention 39
Scottish Council of Churches (later
    Action of Churches Together) 46

Scottish Council of Development and Industry 48
Scottish Covenant (1949) 9, 39
Scottish Covenant Association 38, 40
Scottish Development International 84
Scottish Financial Enterprise 12
Scottish Green Party 66
Scottish Home Rule Association 17, 19, 33–36, 39, 77
Scottish Home Rule Association (reformed 1919) 37
Scottish Investment Bank 12
Scottish Labour Action 49
Scottish Labour League 35
Scottish Labour Party 44, 47–8, 73
Scottish Liberal Association 35
Scottish Liberal Women's Association 35
Scottish National Party 25
    and the 79 Group 60; birth of 34, 39, 77; by-election success 38, 41–43, 50; driving principle behind 25; electoral success 42–3, 72; first MP (R. McIntyre) 38; independence referendums 13–15, 18–21, 59–65, 71, 75, 78, 162–3; losing support (1979) 60; rise in support for (2000s) 41–43, 52, 62, 78
Scottish Office 33
Scottish Parliament
    administrations 59, 61, 152; establishment of 49, 52, 78; history of 32; opening of 42; permanence of 130; proposals for 36
Scottish Parliament Information Centre 66
Scottish Party 39
Scottish Treasury, need for 128–9
Scottish TUC 48
SDP-Liberal Alliance (1981) 47
Secretary for Scotland, post of 33
Section 30 order, requests for 72, 162
79 Group 59–60
79 Group Socialist Society 60
Sewel Convention 130
Shared Rule report 97
Shorthouse, Rob 63
Sillars, Jim 47, 50, 60–1, 71
Sinn Fein 60

Smaill, Peter 57
Smith of Kelvin, Lord 65–6
Smith, Adam 140
Smith, John 9, 48
Smith Commission 14, 66, 69
Social Cohesion Fund 112, 124–5
social security, responsibility for 97
    system in N. Ireland 98
Society of United Irishmen 27
Steel, David (Lord Steel of Aikwood) 47, 52
Steel Commission 47, 52–53, 79
Stevenson, Struan 45
Sturgeon, Nicola 9, 41, 47, 62, 71–2
sub-national debt, funding of 109
subsidiarity, principle of 21, 25, 53, 81–2, 97, 134, 152, 155
Swinney, John 61

tax systems
    centralised 111–2; devolved 114, 116; in Crown dependencies 113; in US states 114–5; income tax 142–3, 149; property tax 144–5; simplified 141; social element of 116; taxes on goods 143
terrorism, policy on 93
Thatcher, Margaret 44, 49, 71, 106
Thomas, R.S. 60
Thomson Review 12
Thorpe, Jeremy 47
Tomkins, Prof. Adam 97
Tone, Wolfe 27
Torrance, David 81
tourism, responsibility for 91
trade and industry, responsibility for 94
transport policy, responsibility for 96
Treason Act (1351) 86
Trench, Alan 58

UK Council of Ministers 133
UK, historical and social links in 123
UK National Air Traffic Service 96
UK Trade and Investment 84
Union with Ireland Act (1800) 32
Unionism, philosophy of 162
universal contributory pension 151
Universal Credit 97

Value Added Tax (VAT) 143–4
Varoufakis, Yanis 121
Victoria, Queen 28
Voltaire 27
Vow, The 63–5, 69

weapons of mass destruction,
    responsibility for 100
West Lothian Question 131
Wilson, Andrew 57

Wilson, Brian 47
Wilson, Gordon 60–1
Wilson, Harold 43, 48
work permits, systems of 91–2
Wright, Canon Kenyon 46
written constitution, need for 52–53, 79,
    118, 130–1, 135, 157

Young Scots League 37
Young Scots Society 35